DEDICATION

The Sandy Cross Conservation Foundation gratefully dedicates this book to Ann and Sandy Cross, in recognition of their generosity, foresight and continuing support.

The Sandy Cross Conservation Foundation, which commissioned the creation of *Paradise Preserved*, is pleased to be able to provide copies of this book free of charge to public libraries and schools across the province. The Foundation thanks the following contributors for their generous support of this book:

 Chevron Canada Resources

 The Calgary Foundation

The Kahanoff Foundation

 Nature Conservancy of Canada

 Canadian Pacific Railway

Alberta Community Development -
Alberta Sport, Recreation, Parks and Wildlife Foundation

The Calgary Foundation - New Sun Fund

The Calgary Foundation – George and Sheila Crawford Flow Through Fund

The Heffring Family, in Memory of Gert and Ed O'Conner

Anonymous

Rob, Ruth Peters and Family

Paradise Preserved

The Ann and Sandy Cross Conservation Area

Text By Bruce Masterman

Photographs by Mike Sturk*

* (unless otherwise indicated)

Bayeux Arts Inc.
119 Stratton Crescent S.W.
Calgary, Alberta, Canada T3H 1T7

National Library of Canada Cataloguing in Publication Data

Masterman, Bruce, 1952-
    Paradise preserved

    Includes index.
    ISBN 1-896209-66-1

    1. Ann and Sandy Cross Conservation Area (Alta.). 2. Wildlife
conservation–Alberta–Calgary Region. 3. Natural resources
conservation areas–Alberta–Calgary Region. I. Title.
QH77.C3M385 2002   333.95'16'09712338   C2001-911672-1

Graphic design: Brian Dyson, Syntax Media Services
Printed in Canada

The publisher gratefully acknowledges the generous support of the Canada
Council for the Arts, the Alberta Foundation for the Arts, and the Government of
Canada through the Book Publishing Industry Development Program.

TABLE OF CONTENTS

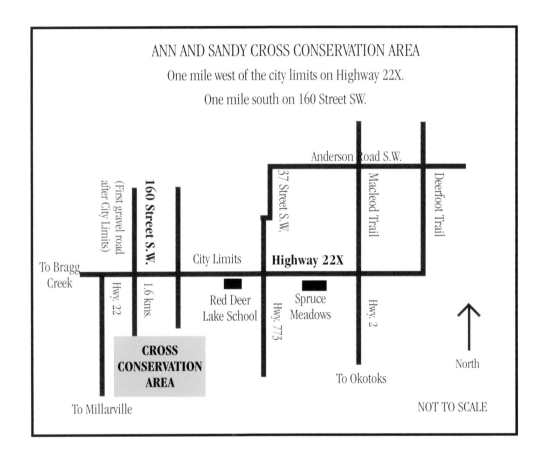

Visitors are asked to arrange visits at least one day in advance by phoning the automated booking line at (403) 931-9001

Foreword
Premier Ralph Klein

Albertans' unparalleled quality of life is due in no small part to the province's unparalleled natural resources. Alberta's strength of character and its spirit have been shaped and inspired by an appreciation and deep sense of connection to the majesty and biodiversity of the provincial landscape.

As Calgary grows it is important that this appreciation and connection be maintained by you and me here today and, perhaps more importantly, by Alberta's children, and their children. It is essential that we have natural areas set aside as living classrooms for future generations.

This is the vision that Ann and Sandy Cross have accomplished through two successive donations of land to the province – and therefore to all Albertans – to create the Ann and Sandy Cross

Conservation Area. The province is extremely grateful to Ann and Sandy for this incredible generosity. Government has been a proud partner in the foundation to manage this wonderful area, and looks forward to participating in future stewardship of the land. The Conservation Area plays an important role in enabling Calgarians of all ages to experience the natural world. I know that the Conservation Area will continue to grow in popularity for students, naturalists, and for those simply seeking a refuge close to home.

The Cross name is linked very strongly to many contributions to the history of this great province. This donation of 4,800 acres to protect this important piece of Alberta's heritage is no exception. It is a magnificent gift to us all. Thank you, Ann and Sandy.

Ralph Klein

A trail in autumn.

Author's Acknowledgements

This book has been a team effort from inception to publication.

For their assistance and support, I wish to acknowledge and express sincere thanks to:

Ann and Sandy Cross, for selflessly providing this special conservation gift for the benefit of future generations. And for making themselves available for more interviews and photographs than they thought necessary.

The board of the Sandy Cross Conservation Foundation, for deciding to tell this important story to the world, and choosing me to help do it.

George Crawford, Tom Beck and Ray Glasrud, who helped mould the original vision of the Conservation Area into reality, and who willingly shared their wisdom with me.

Jacquie Gilson, Reg Rempel, Susan Hayduk and the rest of the devoted Conservation Area staff for their passion and considerable knowledge.

Premier Ralph Klein, for providing the foreword.

Everyone who provided financial support for this book.

Larry Simpson, Ken Carter, Jim Kerr, Arthur Patterson, Eleanor Gillespie, Harry Riva Cambrin, Ralph Nelson, Pat Young and others too numerous to mention for providing special insight that helped round out this story.

Friends and relatives of Ann and Sandy, for sharing details of their lives, especially Sidney Madden and Mary Shakespeare, who welcomed me to the family luncheon on Sandy's 86th birthday.

Olga Droppo, Dick Choy and other Cross Area volunteers, who never stop caring.

My wife, Karen, for her loving support – and those late-night, brutally honest editing sessions — and our wonderful daughters, Sarah and Chelsea, for being there.

Photographer Mike Sturk, who spent many hours roaming the Conservation Area to capture the best images to illustrate this book.

The good folks in the archives section of the Glenbow Museum.

Publisher Ashis Gupta, of Bayeux Arts Inc., for his enthusiasm, patience and expertise.

And, finally, to all Cross Area visitors – young and old alike — who allowed their experiences to become part of this book.
I am extremely grateful to you all.

Bull elk in winter.

Introduction

The Ann and Sandy Cross Conservation Area is a wonderful and multi-faceted story. It is about selfless generosity, Canadian heritage and responsible land stewardship. It is about a vision to protect forever a parcel of 4,800 acres of rolling hills, forest and grassland on the doorstep of a major metropolitan city. This story also is about dedication and shoulder-to-shoulder co-operation between naturalists, conservation organizations, governments and major corporations to ensure birds, animals, plants, wildflowers and trees have a safe place to exist for many, many years to come. And it is about children and adults having a place to learn about nature, and how they can minimize their impact on the natural world.

I began writing about this special area shortly after the announcement in late 1987 that Ann and Sandy Cross had taken 2,000 acres from their Rothney Farm and turned it over to the Alberta government for use as a conservation area. I visited the property on a balmy March afternoon. The land was snow-free; grass rippled in a warm west wind. I met with Tom Beck, a life-long conservationist and volunteer trustee of the Nature Conservancy of Canada, and George Crawford, long-time lawyer and friend of Sandy Cross. Tom and George, along with rancher-biologist Ray Glasrud, were instrumental in turning the Cross vision into reality. Ann and Sandy weren't there. They were still at their second home in Hawaii, where they used to spend the winter. Our meeting took place in a little log cabin, where Sandy had lived alone for three decades before marrying Ann in 1974.

Tom and George spoke with unbridled enthusiasm about the Conservation Area, how it came to be and how Sandy envisioned its future – untouched and free of development. The two men talked of Sandy's love of nature, and how the land donation was contingent on the province agreeing to preserve it in its natural state for wildlife. They spoke of an upcoming open house in the Red Deer Lake community center at which plans for the Conservation Area were to be shared with neighbours and others. "This is a significant event for conservation in Canada," Tom told me. "I hope Albertans see it in that context."

Later, ranch foreman Reg Rempel took me on a tour of the property, patiently posing for a photograph at a hilltop fence line with an amazing view of the Rocky Mountains to the west, and the rapidly approaching city to the northeast. It was on that day in 1988 that the true magnitude of the couple's gift hit me with the force of the legendary Chinook winds that buffet the area in winter. Even then, years before it expanded to 4,800 acres, the Conservation Area was the largest private land donation in Canada. It beckoned people near and far to come and study nature, to learn to appreciate it and recognize the need for areas like this.

As a life-long outdoor enthusiast, I always thought I knew a thing or two about nature. But every time I visit the Conservation Area, I discover how little I really do know. Thankfully, there's never a shortage of people out there eager to share their knowledge with others — even writers. Jacquie Gilson, the project's original general manager, is one of them. She is a veritable fount of knowledge about how things work in the natural world. Jacquie combines her extensive know-how with an infectious passion for the Conservation Area. In conjunction with the board of the Sandy Cross Conservation Foundation, she works with a quiet but steady resolve to ensure that day-to-day operations and future plans stay true to the original vision.

In the past 13 years, I've visited the Conservation Area dozens of times. I once was honoured to tour the land with Sandy Cross, at the time a mere 75. As he steered a bouncing pick-up truck along a maze of rough trails, Sandy eagerly pointed out interesting sights, like the place in a low valley where a former owner had tried to sink a water well. "They finally started looking on the ridges rather than the bottoms and they found water." A fat cigar firmly clenched in his teeth, Sandy nodded towards a dense stand of poplar and spruce trees. "We're probably driving by lots of deer, moose and elk, bedded down in the cool trees," he said calmly, with reverence. Sandy was playing the role of tour guide that day, and he was doing it with the pride of a new father showing off a newborn. It was obvious that the land was a big part of Sandy, much more than just an asset ripe for liquidation. At one point, he gazed in wonder over a field of native grassland waving in the wind, and observed: "I hated the thought of

seeing it built up and bulldozed and made into a real mess. This is the ideal way to preserve it."

During the research for this book, I visited Ann and Sandy for several days in their oceanfront home in Victoria. Sandy was born in the British Columbia capital on April 11, 1914, and spent the first month of his life there before his family returned home to Alberta. Now, Sandy and Ann spend much of their time in Victoria. When I visited them, Sandy showed me around their two-storey house. Their bedroom on the second floor had a huge picture window that offered a spectacular vista of the Pacific Ocean just off their property. In front of the window, two easy chairs flanked a small table on which sat a set of powerful binoculars and wildlife identification guidebooks. "I sit here for hours, watching for whales, seals and sea otters, whatever I'm lucky enough to spot," Sandy told me.

Later, he led me through their carefully maintained garden of flowers and vegetables to a grassy path leading to the driftwood and rock-strewn ocean shoreline. As screaming gulls wheeled overhead and ducks bobbed in the surf, Sandy pointed out the polished boulder where he likes to sit and watch for wildlife. He once saw two mink, weaving with fluid furtiveness through the rocks and washed-up wood on the beach. His face lit up as he told of seeing a mother sea otter and two of her young frolicking in the kelp, the mother floating on her back with the young ones taking turns climbing aboard her stomach. Sandy seemed genuinely disappointed the otters weren't there that day. "We're probably a little early, or maybe they've already been here." He continued scanning the water in vain, eager to share the wildlife from which he derived so much pleasure. For several minutes, we watched in silence as the waves lapped gently onto the shoreline. When we turned to leave, Sandy spied a sun-bleached crab claw lying white against a stone. "Something had a good meal," he observed.

For decades, Sandy watched for wildlife with the same kind of enthusiasm on the wagon trails and hillsides at Rothney Farm. Each coyote, deer or great horned owl he saw was like the very first one. It never failed to elicit fresh wonder in Sandy. His love of nature is a big part of Sandy — no matter if he's in the foothills of southern Alberta or on Vancouver Island.

Many people who frequent the Conservation Area that bears Sandy and Ann's name share that feeling. On a late-spring Saturday several years ago, I took a church youth group there. Amazed, I listened as volunteer naturalist Olga Droppo reeled off the common and scientific names of plants and flowers I never knew existed. Olga pointed out animal tracks in the dirt and nests that we otherwise wouldn't have noticed. At one point, she suddenly stopped walking, tipped her head and announced: "Can you hear that? A Townsend's solitaire. It's celebrating spring."

During lunch break, I spied a teenaged girl from our group sitting alone on a hillside overlooking Pine Creek valley, studying the distant mountains and trees below her. "This is so beautiful," she said, in a low voice resonating with awe and respect. Many thousands of visitors to the Area since it opened to the public in 1991 would agree wholeheartedly. I've had the opportunity to talk with many of them, in formal interviews and casual trailside chats. I've heard the passion in their voices and seen the excitement on their faces. I keep coming back to this special area, whether it's to hike for pleasure, take photographs or to do research for my writing.

Journalists aren't supposed to become fans of the subjects on which they write. Sometimes, however, it just happens. This journalist makes no apologies for becoming an unabashed supporter of the Ann and Sandy Cross Conservation Area. The magic it casts is strong, the story almost too good to be true. I've written thousands of published words about the area, and consider myself blessed to have been given the opportunity to write thousands more in this book. I hope, with all my heart, that feeling is reflected in the pages that follow.

Bruce Masterman, High River, Alberta

Chapter One
The Land Connection

"Wonder, reverence, the feeling that one is nearer the mystery of things – that is what one feels in places of such sublime beauty."
James B. Harkin, first commissioner of Parks Canada (then known as the Dominion Parks Branch)

"I liked how you could hear the leaves rustle together and it sounded like a river. I liked how it was so quiet. I liked the tall grass."
Kelsi, student, Eugene Coste Elementary School

It is spring 1945. The snow-capped craggy peaks of the Rocky Mountains extend for hundreds of kilometers on the western horizon. In the foreground, the grass of the foothills is like a soft lush carpet, rolling gently and invitingly eastward. Patches of willows and poplar forests punctuate the landscape, splashes of contrasting shades of brown against a natural canvas of greens and yellows. Prairie crocuses are sprouting fuzzy mauve flowers on hilltops covered with native prairie grasses. On one of those hills stands a man, small in stature and feeling a little more humbled with each passing minute.

Sandy Cross gazes over the vista spread out before him, his blue eyes scanning the mountains to pick out peaks with familiar names

Paradise Preserved

Sandy's father, A.E. Cross, in photo taken in 1899.
(Photo: Glenbow Archives NA-165-4)

like Coffin, Livingston, Plateau, Burke and Hailstone Butte. He turns and peers to the northeast. The city of Calgary is but a mere spot in the distance. Sandy shakes his head, finding it hard to believe that almost 98,000 people have settled there since his grandfather helped establish the city at the confluence of the Bow and Elbow rivers just 70 years earlier. Where did they all come from, he wonders, and how big can the city possibly get? Turning his view once again to the west, Sandy stares in wonder at the mountains and hills, then peers south to take in the Pine Creek valley bisecting the northern part of the property from east to west. Some of the fields have been cultivated, but most of the land is just as it was a century ago. Sandy's mind begins journeying back in time, back to another special place, the home of his youth in the Porcupine Hills west of Nanton. He smiles. The land spread out before him reminds him so much of the A7 Ranche, founded in 1886 by his father, Alfred Ernest (A.E.) Cross. Like the A7, this property also was home to deer, elk, moose, coyotes and hawks – wildlife Sandy had learned to respect and loved to watch ever since he was a kid. Who would have thought, Sandy wonders, that there could be wild creatures and undeveloped rangeland, hills and forests like this so close to Calgary?

At that moment, just weeks after his thirty-first birthday, the bachelor made a decision that would change his life — and eventually the lives of thousands of others several decades later. Sandy Cross bought two sections (1,280 acres) of that ranchland for the princely sum of $30 an acre. He named it Rothney Farm, after his mother, Helen Rothney Macleod Cross, the oldest of five children born to Colonel James Macleod and his wife, Mary Isabelle Drever. Sandy Cross started raising shorthorn cattle, a breed which his father had admired and respected dating back to when he homesteaded the A7. In the ensuing years, Sandy acquired more land until Rothney Farm grew to nine sections (5,760 acres) by the 1980's.

Sandy's mother, Helen Rothney Macleod Cross, in her wedding dress in Calgary in 1899.
(Photo: Glenbow Archives NA-2536-4)

But Sandy never set out with the intention of being what some would consider a land baron. All he'd wanted was some property to call his own, land he could share with the wildlife he'd come to love as a boy, land on which he could raise a few cattle and explore on horseback and on foot. Considering his family's history, that expectation seemed more than reasonable. Respect and appreciation for the land, and for traditional Western values and heritage, ran thick in the family's blood.

His Scottish-born grandfather, Colonel James Farquharson Macleod, had come west from Toronto in 1870 with the North-West Mounted Police to quell the rebellion led by Louis Riel in the Rupert's Land district of what became Manitoba. In 1876, Macleod's life was marked by two important events: his marriage to Mary Isabelle Drever, the daughter of a trader with the Hudson's Bay fur-trading company, and his appointment as commissioner of the North-West Mounted Police. Macleod's main duty was to keep the peace between the growing number of settlers and resident Indians in the districts of Alberta and Saskatchewan. The town of Fort Macleod was named after him, and Macleod sent a troop to establish what was then known as Fort Calgary.

Macleod developed a fondness for this undeveloped new region, and cultivated the friendship and respect of the native people. As a result, the Canadian government in 1877 chose Macleod to bring together several Indian bands —Blackfoot, Cree and Stony — on the banks of the Bow River at Blackfoot Crossing downstream of Fort Calgary. There, he and David Laird, first lieutenant-governor of the Northwest Territories, negotiated with Chief Crowfoot, of the Blackfoot Confederacy, and other Indian leaders to sign what became known as Treaty 7. The treaty ended the Indians' traditional role as free-roaming hunters and gatherers by restricting them to reserves. The government would pay them regularly, establish schools and teach them agricultural methods. Mary Macleod and

Sandy (far left) and his siblings (from left to right) Mary, John, James and Margaret pose on a hay wagon on the A7 Ranch circa 1920.
(Photo: Glenbow Archives NA-691-3)

five other white women signed the treaty as witnesses. The treaty cleared the way for the railway west, and opened the opportunity for settlement.

In 1878, Mary Macleod gave birth to their first child. Baptized

When Sandy started assembling Rothney Farm in 1945, it reminded him of the A7 Ranche, west of Nanton, shown here in a 1927 photograph.
(Photo: Glenbow Archives NA-857-1)

Helen Rothney Macleod – but more commonly known as Nell or Nellie – she was the first white baby born in the region. Helen was the oldest of five children. When Helen was just six years old, her future husband, Alfred Ernest Cross, decided to leave his home in Montreal to follow the westward development of the Canadian Pacific Railway. His father, Alexander, was a judge in the appeals court of Quebec. Ernest, the fourth of seven children, was just 22 when he rode the train into Calgary in 1884. Before leaving Montreal, he'd been schooled for eight years in business, agriculture, medicine and veterinary medicine.

A.E. worked almost two years as bookkeeper and veterinarian at the Cochrane Ranche west of Calgary before leaving to homestead west of Nanton. That first winter, he lost 19 of 20 head of shorthorn cattle in a blizzard. The sole survivor was Maggie the 13th, a milk cow who was tied in a shed during the storm. That incident kicked off the Cross family's long-standing devotion to the breed. The A7, which is today operated by one of A.E.'s grandsons, is the longest-running family-operated ranch in Canada.

Fate intervened in 1891 when A.E. was injured by a saddle horn while riding a bucking horse on the A7. While recuperating back in

Mule deer doe in poplar trees.

Montreal, his doctor advised him to stay away from horses and the remote ranch in the foothills west of Nanton. Looking for other opportunities, but wishing to stay in the West he now considered home, A.E. decided to start a brewery. After a year spent learning the brewing business in Montreal, he returned to Calgary in 1892 and launched the Calgary Brewing and Malting Co. Ltd., the first brewery in the Northwest Territories. The brewery's logo – a buffalo head framed by a horseshoe imprinted with the name Calgary – became a well-known symbol of the family-owned business.

A.E. remained president until his death in 1932. During his era, the brewery also owned or leased about 50 hotels in Western Canada, providing a ready and thirsty market for its golden liquid product. A.E. also helped found Calgary's exclusive private Ranchmen's Club and the Western Stock Growers Association, served as a member of the Territorial Assembly, helped form the Calgary Exhibition Association and was one of the so-called Big Four ranchers who bankrolled the first Calgary Stampede in 1912. In his spare time, he bred polo horses and was himself proficient at the sport. Although not widely recognized for it, A.E. also was instrumental in establishing Alberta's oil and gas industry. He started Calgary Petroleum Products in 1912, and was a director of Canadian Western Natural Gas. A.E.'s fortunes rose even further in 1924 when Royalite Oil Company, for which he served on the board of directors, hit a major oil strike in Turner Valley. A.E. also became

Left: A weather-worn building near the old Stewart Barn.
Right: The old Stewart Barn in autumn.

Close-up of window at old Stewart Barn.

known as one of the first ranchers to develop a planned crossbreeding program using Shorthorn and Hereford bulls.

Writer Catherine Philip described the origin of the relationship between A.E. Cross and Helen (Nell) Rothney Macleod in a story published in Chatelaine magazine in July 1965. The couple first met in 1894 when her father introduced them while they walked to his office in the courthouse in Calgary. Col. Macleod died several months after that inaugural meeting. Helen and A.E. met for the second time in 1899 during a race at a gymkhana, a fun competition played out on horseback. They teamed up to win a needle-and-thread race, which involved women waiting at one end of the course, with the men at the other. At a signal, the men would mount their horses and gallop to their partner. There they would dismount, while the man handed the woman a needle to thread. Then he would swing her onto the horse and race back to the start. The relationship blossomed between the community's most eligible bachelor and Nell, who had been working as a cashier in the Hudson's Bay Company store after the death of her father left her mother and siblings in dire financial straits. A.E. and Helen were well suited to each other, since both were of Scottish descent and shared a fierce independence common to their pioneer backgrounds.

After they married in June 1899, the couple moved into a wood-frame house at 1240 8th Avenue S.E. in Calgary, near the south entrance of what became the Calgary Zoo. Over the next several

Old wooden-wheeled equipment in a snowy field; a reminder of days gone by.

An old weathered house near the Stewart Barn shows signs of age.

years, Helen and A.E. had seven children: James; Mary (Dover); Margaret (Shakespeare), known as Marmo; Sandy (who was baptized Alexander Rothney); John; Helen; and Selkirk. Toddlers Helen and Selkirk both died of diphtheria in 1904. Sandy, who was born April 11, 1914, is the last surviving child.

The family divided its time between the A7 Ranche and their stately house beside the Bow River. It was a convenient spot, since A.E. could walk between home and brewery. The household's trappings included Colonel Macleod's medicine chest, A.E.'s polo mallets and a buffalo skull that one of the kids had found on the A7. When she wasn't busy raising her family, Nell found time to help establish and volunteer for the local chapter of the Canadian Women's Club, the Cathedral Church of the Redeemer and the Southern Alberta Oldtimer's Association. She also was Dominion president of the International Order of Daughters of the Empire (IODE).

Sandy, the second oldest son, was younger than Jim by 11 years, Mary by nine years and

Ruffed grouse.

Margaret by two years. John, born two years after Sandy, was the youngest. Sandy spent many years attending school outside of Alberta, including six years at Appleby College near Oakville, Ontario, a year at Royal Military College and one year in Chicago.

But it was his time on the A7 Ranche that Sandy remembers with the most affection. He rode horseback over the hills, and explored the land on foot, often alone. He recalls his mother having a good eye for spotting wildlife, and proficiency in controlling the local gopher population with a .22 rifle. One time, when Sandy was eight or ten, he and his mother went for a walk through a field of knee-high native grass. Suddenly Helen stopped, walked over to a thick clump of grass, crouched down and gently spread it open with her hands, revealing a nest made by a Western meadowlark. Inside were several eggs. Sandy was impressed with his mother's keen eye, since he would never have known it was there. He credits her with helping shape his own interest in wildlife. Sandy loved hearing her stories of growing up near southern Alberta natives, learning their ways and their language. Helen Cross was fluent in Blackfoot and Peigan. "She was a great woman," Sandy says.

Sandy, and the rest of his siblings, also held their father in high respect. The patriarch's strong personality and keen interest in everything he did – from ranching and mining to cattle and beer – deeply touched the middle son. But no matter what venture he tackled, A.E. did it quietly, without fanfare and without seeking any kind of public recognition. He disdained publicity, often telling Sandy that a man should be judged by the results of his work, not the noise he makes while doing it. His mother shared that attitude. "Neither of them ever grew above themselves and what they'd done," Sandy recalls. "It was hard to get anything out of them if you wanted them to talk about themselves." Not surprisingly, Sandy is the same way.

Of the three sons, Sandy generally kept the lowest public profile and exhibited the mildest temperament. Jim ruled the brewery and was heavily involved in the Calgary Exhibition and Stampede. And John was fairly outgoing, a tradition-hugging rancher who had a high profile in the cattle industry, including the presidency of the Alberta Cattle Breeders' Association. Sister Mary Dover, who once ran unsuccessfully for the provincial Liberals, was in the public eye as a city alderman, army officer and heritage preservationist.

In his late teens, Sandy had a dream of heading north to search for gold in the Yukon. Although he enjoyed brief sojourns to the Yukon, the life of a prospector was not in the cards for Sandy. Instead, the brewery beckoned. Older brother, Jim, had taken over as president in 1932 when A.E. died, leaving the brewery to his three sons. Jim asked Sandy to come on as brew master, and Sandy reluctantly agreed. As a result, he switched university courses from mining engineering to chemical engineering, receiving his degree from the University of Alberta. Sandy joined the brewery in 1935 and stayed there until it was sold to a national corporation in 1961. The three brothers also held joint ownership of the A7 Ranche after their father's death. John managed it on their behalf until 1963, when he bought out the interests of Sandy and Jim.

While he worked at the brewery, Sandy lived with his widowed mother in the family house beside the Bow River until her death in 1959. He spent much of his time off at the A7. After starting Rothney Farm in 1945, he often stayed in a one-room spruce log cabin built in 1930. That cabin still stands today, serving as a ranch office. Considered a loner by many, Sandy developed a legendary reputation as an eclectic character and prankster. Part of his reputation was based on his self-described affection for the product he was in charge of turning out at the Calgary brewery. Today, Sandy doesn't touch alcohol.

Several decades ago, Sandy was a good friend with a couple who owned a house in the high-class neighbourhood of Pump Hill, near the Glenmore Reservoir. The woman made the mistake of telling Sandy she wouldn't mind keeping a pig on their property. Sandy knew her husband didn't share the same ambition. One day, Sandy visited another friend who lived on a 25-acre parcel near the present site of the Chinook Shopping Mall. The friend, who also happened to work as a gardener at the A7, owned a sow that had recently produced a litter of piglets. Sandy promptly bought one of the piglets. One dark evening, he set out to deliver it. The little pig was in a burlap sack, with a hole cut out of one end so its head was free. Sandy placed the piglet on the front seat of his car, and held it firmly with one hand while he drove with the other.

By the time he arrived at the couple's house, the piglet had managed to get its front hooves through the head hole as it struggled desperately to get free. Sandy was surprised to discover many fancy cars parked outside the brightly lit house. Apparently Calgary's high society had gathered for a party. Laughter and the sound of clinking glasses inside the house seemed to heighten the urgency of the wriggling piglet's panicked squeals as Sandy carried it towards the front door. Passing through an outside door into a screened veranda, Sandy briefly considered releasing the piglet in the porch. But he feared it would bolt to freedom when somebody opened the door. So he opened the inner main door, instantly spied several wide-eyed revelers and quickly released the pig on the lush carpet. As Sandy fled back to his car to make good his getaway, he chuckled at the chorus of shouts and panicked cries inside the house as the piglet dodged between legs and under tables and chairs. Decades later, Sandy's eyes still twinkle and a mischievous grin creases his face while recounting the caper. "I heard later they had a hell of a time catching that poor little pig."

Sandy was famous for having animals in his vehicles, some alive and some decidedly not. Longtime friend Jock Gourley tells of the time when Sandy was driving to work after a particularly fun-filled weekend with friends. Hearing a strange noise in the rear end of his car, he pulled into a gas station near the brewery. Sandy told the attendant he could hear hissing and thought he was getting a flat tire. Both men circled the car but could see nothing wrong. Then the hissing started again. Sandy opened the trunk and discovered three rather distressed geese. "You wring their necks," Sandy told the attendant. "Keep two and give one to your friend."

Passengers in Sandy's cars and trucks often had to share a seat with a chicken, or a pig. During bird-hunting season, Sandy once placed a dead pheasant in the car and promptly forgot about it. He was rudely reminded some weeks later when a rather unpleasant odor permeated throughout the vehicle. Sandy's niece, Sidney Madden, one of three daughters of his late sister Marmo, recalls as a young girl driving with her uncle late one autumn in the Bassano district. Sandy spotted a dead duck lying beside the road. He pulled over, picked up the frozen fowl and tossed it in the trunk. At home, they thawed it for three hours and cooked it for supper. "It was delicious," Sidney recounts.

Although a man of considerable means, Sandy is famous for not showing it. "Whenever you saw Sandy, you'd feel he didn't have five cents to his name," says Arthur Patterson, who became a neighbour and friend when Sandy established Rothney Farm. Since his birth in 1913, Patterson has lived on a farm just south of Sandy's property. He notes Sandy never put on airs or dressed like a wealthy man. At bull sales and other public places, Sandy was likely

Stewart Barn in winter.

to show up in jeans, running shoes, blaze orange hunting coat and a floppy fishing hat. One time in Montreal, he was wearing a ranch-style down vest when he tried to book a room in a ritzy hotel. The desk clerk snobbishly asked if he could afford to stay there. Sandy hastily departed for another less snobbish hotel.

Arthur Patterson remembers his neighbour as always behaving like a gentleman, extremely polite and well spoken. Although he supported various community affairs by donating to school and hall projects, he steadfastly declined any offer of recognition in return for his good deeds. Just six months older than Sandy, Arthur Patterson used to visit his neighbour in the log cabin on Rothney Farm. Patterson himself had hauled in the logs to build it in 1930. At

Sandy's 80th birthday party, the musically-gifted Patterson – who's "blind in one eye and can't see out the other" – cheerfully played "For He's a Jolly Good Fellow" on his harmonica.

It became apparent that Sandy had learned much about the livestock industry from his father. In relatively short order, Rothney Farm gained the respect of cattlemen for bringing and buying prime stock at the annual Calgary Bull Sale. Sandy traveled regularly to Scotland in search of top breeding shorthorn bulls, such as Calrossie Highland Piper for which he paid a whopping $30,000 in 1952. Piper was Sandy's main herd bull for five seasons. Other great bulls owned by Sandy included Rothney Juggler, Rothney Kinross, Bapton Cairnbrogie, Rothney Illustrious, Rothney Wildfire and Rothney Idol.

Sandy enjoyed showing his cattle, and the land, to anyone who expressed an interest. Indeed, there's a lot to show – and much of it is wild. The aspen forest and grasslands are home to more than 300 plant species, and wildlife from deer mouse to moose, great gray owls to pileated woodpeckers. The area supports the highest concentration of red-tailed hawks in North America. Sandy's niece, Jane Shakespeare Horner, a daughter of his sister Marmo, grew up in Vancouver but regularly came to Rothney Farm to visit. "I still get a lump in my throat when I drive into the countryside south of Calgary," says Jane. "Sandy loved that foothills country and so did our mother Marmo." Tragically, Marmo and her husband, Vancouver lawyer John Sidney Shakespeare, died in a car crash in 1979.

Sandy would drive Jane around the farm in a pickup truck, along with a yellow Labrador retriever named Kika. A gift from Marmo, the dog was named after the only Peigan word Sandy remembers his mother ever uttering while the kids were growing up. And she said it often. Kika means keep quiet. Bouncing along a two-rut trail through fields, creek valley and forests, Sandy was constantly on the lookout for birds and coyotes. He'd identify hawks by species and speculate to Jane what kind of season each one was having. Sandy delighted in pointing out birds that Jane would never have seen.

David Dover, son of Mary and her husband Melville, spent a lot of time with his uncle Sandy while he was growing up. Sometimes Sandy would take him to work at the brewery, where David was surprised to see how much the employees respected him. But David's most cherished memories are from times he spent with his uncle at Rothney Farm and at the A7. At the farm, Sandy would put David in the cab of his big Caterpillar tractor and drive around the farm, feeding cattle and seeing the sights. David also rode the hills on his polo horse, a thoroughbred gelding named Cymbalene. Sometimes he'd help out by moving cattle or haying and stooking – once a common process of piling hay to dry. As far back as the early 1960's, Sandy shared with his nephew a concern that Rothney Farm one day would be split up into small parcels and developed as rural housing. Sandy's vision to preserve it was starting to germinate.

While spending his boyhood years at the A7 Ranche in the Porcupine Hills, Sandy became friends with a neighbouring rancher named Slim Sonnie and his family. Sandy called him the Pennsylvania Swede, because he grew up in that state and his roots were in Sweden. Slim's daughter, Eleanor Gillespie, says a life-long friendship sprouted between herself and Sandy, despite a 16-year age difference. Sandy used to show her his many books on wildlife. "He always noticed nature."

One summer day almost a half century ago, Sandy invited Eleanor to come north to spend a day riding horseback on his new farm in the foothills. She readily accepted. Eleanor was eager to see what her childhood friend had made of himself. They had a good day exploring the property, but Eleanor couldn't shake the feeling that Sandy had made an unwise purchase. Instead of miles and miles of rolling open pastureland such as on the A7 and adjacent ranchland in the Porcupine Hills, much of Rothney Farm was covered in willow and forest. "I thought it was just a brush pile," opines Eleanor, who ranches with her husband and sons along the Red Deer River in eastern Alberta. "Right then, I couldn't see any good in it." When she offered her opinion to Sandy, he just smiled and looked around him. "You never know," he replied, with a characteristic twinkle in his eye. "It might just be worth something some day."

Those words proved to be ironically prophetic. One day, the land *was* worth something, millions of dollars in fact. But rather

Ann and Sandy Cross pose on a hillside at the Conservation Area.

than exploit it for the profit he once talked of over a saddle horn with a skeptical friend, Sandy chose to give most of it away in order to preserve it long into the future.

An inquisitive badger. (Brian Wolitski photo)

Chapter 2
Building the Legacy

"Our land is more valuable than your money. It will last forever. It will not perish as long as the sun shines and the water flows, and through all the years it will give life to men and beasts. It was put there by the Great Spirit and we cannot sell it because it does not belong to us."
Chief Crowfoot, Chief of Blackfoot Nation

"I loved the deer and the birds in their natural habitat."
Breanna, student, A.E. Bowers Elementary School

There wasn't much that Jim Kerr didn't come to know about the Cross boys. Oldest brother J.B. (Jim) Cross hired Kerr after the Second World War to be the chief accountant of the Calgary Brewing and Malting Company. Kerr wasn't too familiar with the Cross family when he came on staff. However, Jim Kerr soon became well acquainted with the financial situation at the brewery and the 50 hotels the brewery owned or leased. He worked daily with J.B. and Sandy, the brew master, sometimes taking out-of-town business trips with them. In ensuing years, Kerr became involved in managing the wide-ranging business interests of Sandy, J.B. and John. Eventually, Kerr's relationship with the brothers evolved from trusted work colleague to close friend of the family.

That's why, in 1973, Jim Kerr felt comfortable putting a proposition to Sandy Cross. Kerr knew Sandy traveled often to Scotland to purchase shorthorn bulls for his breeding operation at Rothney Farm. Kerr's father had died earlier that year, and he was eager to travel to Scotland to see an aged aunt, his only surviving relative. So Kerr thought it made perfect sense to ask Sandy if he could travel with him on his next trip to Scotland. "Heavens no!" Sandy replied. "I'm getting married soon." The news came as a total surprise to Kerr and just about everybody else who knew Sandy.

After all, the middle Cross son was 59 and a committed bachelor. While his two brothers and two sisters had been busy getting married and having children, Sandy had enjoyed a carefree single life: hanging out in hotel beer parlours with colorful characters with names such as Rattlesnake Pete, hunting birds, skiing, making the odd trip to the Yukon and overseeing operations of his beloved Rothney Farm. Now, Sandy was getting married. The popular thinking of the day was that whoever caught Sandy's heart must be a remarkable person. She is.

Ann Abbott is vivacious, with a sharp wit and mind to match. The daughter of Polish immigrants, she was born October 9th, 1920 in North Battleford, Saskatchewan. During the challenging days of the Dirty Thirties, her parents moved their large family to a farm, where they raised cattle and grew crops. Up until Grade 8, Ann walked 10 kilometers round-trip each day to a one-room schoolhouse. Ann regularly rode bareback on the family horse,

Nancy, to pick up the mail at the post office several kilometers away. When the spirited mare became tired, she seemed to make a game of knocking the accomplished young rider off into streams or onto the ground. Ann took it all in stride.

Ann moved back into Battleford when she started Grade 10. After high school, she went south to Regina to train to be a nurse and later became a lab technician. In Regina, Ann met and married her first husband, Brian Abbott, a chartered accountant who later ventured into the oil business. Together, they had five children. The Abbott's moved to Calgary around 1953. Tragedy struck the family soon after, when Brian died of a stroke at the age of 42. Ann was left with five children ages one to 12.

With such a large family to raise on her own, Ann decided to stay at home rather than take a full-time job outside the house. While the kids were asleep or at school, she successfully played the stock market.

Ann had been a widow for fourteen years when she met Sandy on a hiking trip organized by mutual friends in Banff National Park. They hit if off from the start. Ann was impressed by Sandy's "old-fashioned" manners, his self-deprecating humour, soft and polite way of speaking, and the respect he showed for her. "He was such a nice guy. Sandy never had airs and he was well-liked by everybody." Ann recalls she was "astounded" that a man who'd been a bachelor for so many years would be even remotely interested in a woman with five kids.

A younger Sandy Cross poses in front of his log cabin on Rothney Farm (circa 1957).
(Photo courtesy of Sandy Cross)

She was blissfully unaware of the Cross family's significant role in Alberta's heritage, and Sandy didn't talk about it. Ann knew a little about Sandy's oldest sister, Mary Dover, only because she'd read newspaper accounts about the feisty city alderman. After Ann and Brian Abbott had moved to Calgary, they'd attended a bull sale at the Stampede grounds. In the crowded arena, Brian pointed out Sandy to Ann, and told her "this man Cross" came from a long line of cattlemen. At the comment, Ann recalls thinking to herself, "So what?" Ann and Sandy were married on January 18th, 1974.

From the perspective of an outsider looking in, life for the

Interior shot of log cabin at Rothney Farm.

newlyweds was anything but high on the hog. The couple moved into the simple but cozy spruce log cabin in the main yard at Rothney Farm. It was full of original paintings by famous artists Nicolas de Grandmaison and Charlie Russell. The walls couldn't hold them all. Hundreds of thousands of dollars' worth of artwork were on the floor, casually propped up against the wall. Ann recalls she "had 22 Indians staring down at me all the time." The paintings are now displayed properly and prominently at the Glenbow Museum in Calgary.

Before Ann and Sandy moved in, the cabin had been expanded from the original 20 by 30-foot one-room structure. The main room, floored with hardwood, includes a small kitchen, complete with a vintage Frigidaire stove and refrigerator. The living room featured a huge fireplace with hearth made of stone. In the addition are a bedroom, cold concrete basement and small bathroom, complete with green striped wallpaper and a wall-mounted sink.

A simple wooden bookshelf set into a wall contains older hardcover volumes with titles such as *Thermo-Dynamics*, *Elements of Chemical Engineering* – with Sandy's name and the date October 1937 inscribed inside the front cover – and *Micro-Organisms and Fermentation*. Hanging on the wall in the concrete basement is an old black and white photograph of J.B. Cross and his mother, Helen. It was taken at a ceremony in 1947 laying a cornerstone at the old brewery in memory of her late husband and brewery founder, A.E. Cross.

Ann and Sandy Cross on their wedding day, January 18, 1974, outside Christ Church, east of Millarville. (Photo courtesy of Ann and Sandy Cross)

A northern flicker on a poplar tree.

In Sandy's bachelor days, he happily called this cabin home. So it seemed only natural that he would want to move his new bride into the cabin in the winter of 1974. But to Ann, it was like moving into "a cabin at the lake. It wasn't uncomfortable, but it was small." Fortunately, almost immediately, the couple approved plans for a larger new house to be built on the west side of Rothney Farm, just east of Highway 22. After one year of living in their cramped quarters, they moved into the spanking new two-storey house. For Ann, the move didn't happen a moment too soon; she was becoming rather claustrophobic.

That spring, they planted 320 young poplars and other trees. It was backbreaking work, prompting Ann to later ask Sandy why the farmhands couldn't have done it. Sandy replied he didn't want them doing "personal" jobs when they had plenty to keep them busy in the fields and with the cattle. Sandy plowed up a large garden in their yard, and then hoed the rows in advance of Ann planting peas and radishes. Sandy himself planted rows of potatoes. He gave Ann a quarter horse and together they would ride all over the property, which by now sprawled over 5,760 acres (2,331 hectares). Sometimes they used their horses to move cattle.

Sandy's pride in the land was obvious. He enjoyed showing it off, but in a loving, respectful way, not a boastful one. He seemed to find personal refuge in the hidden glades, watering holes and other places where he could secretly watch wildlife go about their normal

American goldfinch on wire fence.

lives. Former neighbour Jock Gourley recalls Sandy's amazing ability to "talk" to coyotes. On a clear night, Sandy loved to mimic the yip-yipping howl of a coyote, just to hear one reply in the distance. If pressed, Sandy today will say coyotes have more brains than people. "He's got a real love of nature, a real sense of it," notes veteran Calgary lawyer George Crawford, a longtime friend, adviser and neighbour.

Sandy has many special memories of the wildlife on Rothney Farm. Like the time a coyote, tenderly carrying a pup in its mouth, crossed the north end of a field, and then backtracked along the field's south part to confuse any predators. The coyote traveled this route eight times until all its pups were safely bedded in a new den. One spring, Sandy surprised a doe and her two white-spotted fawns still wet from birth. Sandy was on horseback another day when he encountered a black bear and her cub at very close quarters. The sow reared up on its hind legs. Sandy thought it looked big enough to be a grizzly. He breathed a deep sigh of relief when the sow dropped to all fours, turned and led its cub away.

Almost as much as seeing the wildlife on his land for himself, Sandy enjoyed hearing about their exploits from others. Reg Rempel, the manager of Rothney Farm since 1984, says talk of wildlife often hijacked regular Saturday morning business meetings involving Sandy, accountant Jim Kerr and himself. The meetings were held in the living room of the log cabin. On the west-facing couch where he always sat, Sandy had a clear view out the two main windows. His attention often seemed to be more on what was happening outside. In that room they assembled, every Saturday morning for many years, to solemnly discuss cattle and hay prices, bovine ailments, the land's carrying capacity for grazing, the weather and other mundane but important topics.

However, the mood in the room changed abruptly if Rempel let slip that he'd seen a long-tailed weasel in the yard, a herd of elk on a hillside or a beaver swimming in Pine Creek. Jim Kerr would roll his eyes and sit back in his chair, resigned to the fact that the business portion of the meeting had just ended. Sandy would sit upright on the edge of his seat, his eyes sparkling with interest, and proceed to pepper Rempel with questions: What exactly was the weasel doing? What colour was it? Which way was it traveling? How many elk were there? Did they look healthy? Had Reg seen any young beaver? Sandy's genuine interest in the land beyond the grass and cattle never ceased to impress Rempel.

He recalls that if Sandy thought the land was being grazed too heavily, he would call in a cattle liner and have some of the cattle hauled off for slaughter. One time, Sandy suddenly decided to ship out 200 cattle – a number he deemed was contributing to over-grazing — and sold them at a low commercial price rather than "sacrifice" the land by keeping them grazing on it. Sandy often expressed regret to Rempel that he had allowed some of the land to

Reg Rempel, manager of Rothney Farm, with cattle.

be cultivated rather than saving more of the native grasses. To this day, much of the land remains unbroken, with 50 per cent in forest. Only eight per cent of the land is native grass, with some encroachment by tame grasses.

When Sandy bought the land, there was evidence of prior human use, likely dating back to the late 1880's. Wagon trails criss-crossed the property and there were remains of two homesteads. On one of them, all that remained was a ramshackle barn. According to legend, the house had been moved to another location in an unsuccessful attempt to remove the ghosts that apparently haunted it. The house was later burned to discourage trespassers. The barn has since been removed. A second homestead – the Stewart place — is located south of the present-day entrance to the Conservation Area. A weathered, two-storey barn still stands beside Pine Creek.

Sandy isn't loud or boisterous – quite the contrary – but his sense of humour is legendary. One day, he was showing friend Ken

Carter, a trust officer with Royal Trust, around his farm. Sandy was driving a four-wheel-drive truck, while Ken and his wife, Betty, followed in their shiny white 1983 Oldsmobile Cutlass two-door coupe. They bounced over old wagon trails, dodging fallen trees and hitting just about every pothole and exposed tree root they encountered. As they returned to the main house to join Ann for a cup of tea, Sandy drove through a deep mud hole in the middle of the trail and emerged easily on the other side.

Carter, a little nervous, stopped just before the muddy spot. Sandy got out of his truck and urged Carter to drive through it. Carter was worried, but knew he could trust Sandy. With Betty urging her husband not to try it, Carter slipped the Olds in gear and inched forward. As the car entered the mud, the bottom seemed to fall out of the hole. The car dropped into the mud and wouldn't move. Murky water rose to the bottom of the car doors. Mud and water sprayed everywhere as Carter stepped on the gas to try to break free. The car wouldn't budge.

Sandy started to laugh and called Carter a "city slicker." Betty was busy shooting her husband "I told you so" looks and questioning his decision to try to drive through the hole. Sandy readily winched out the now not-so-shiny Olds and they carried on to teatime. "We'll call that Carter's Mudhole from now on," Sandy announced to his red-faced friend. Carter says he never again trusted Sandy's advice when it came to driving.

In the early days of their marriage, Ann became familiar with Sandy's generosity – not just with family members but also total strangers. He selflessly and quietly shared his wealth with any individual or group that he deemed worthy. The word "No" didn't seem to be part of his vocabulary when it came to helping others, especially if it was a cash-strapped artist or a hopeful gold prospector in need of a stake.

Sandy regularly donated money to a variety of community causes, including area First Nations reserves, a gymnasium project at Strathcona-Tweedsmuir School, local churches, the Western Heritage Centre at Cochrane and Camp Kiwanis, a camp for under-privileged kids near Bragg Creek. Sandy brushes off suggestions that his philanthropy is worthy of recognition. "If it hadn't been for my

Sandy Cross also donated land to the University of Calgary for the Rothney Astrophysical Observatory.

father leaving me some money, I wouldn't have been able to do a lot of those things," he says. "The credit should go to him, whatever little things I've done."

Members of local First Nations bands often showed up at Ann and Sandy's doorstep, offering to sell some piece of traditional clothing, artwork or other artifacts for which the couple had no practical use. But Sandy was always eager to help out, and soon the house was cluttered with items they couldn't use.

Sandy's empathy with First Nations people can be traced back as far as 1877, when his grandfather Col. James Macleod helped negotiate Treaty 7. The government had assigned Macleod because Chief Crowfoot and the others trusted him for protecting them against white settlers and stopping the flow of whisky that was devastating their people. "The Mounted Police have protected us as the feathers of the bird protect it from the frosts of winter," Chief Crowfoot said. "I wish all my people good, and trust that our hearts will increase in goodness from this time forward. I will sign the treaty."

The treaty sent the natives to live on reserves, opening the rest of the land – where they had once freely roamed and hunted — to be settled by white people moving West. Many came by the railroad that the treaty had made possible. According to Sandy, his grandfather believed to his death in 1894 that he had betrayed his native friends. Macleod's oldest daughter — Sandy's mother —

A porcupine shows its teeth while gnawing on an aspen tree.

used to share stories around the family supper table about her father's feelings of guilt. Sandy believes that's why he's chosen to support members of the First Nations. "I guess I do get worked up, or have done so over the years," he says. "See, it must be all linked together. I never really realized it was."

A major beneficiary of Sandy's generous nature was the University of Calgary, which operates the Rothney Astrophysical Observatory on land that Sandy donated in the early 1970's. Alan Clark, a British-born professor with the U of C's physics department, started looking in 1970 for a site for a new observatory, a place close to Calgary where students could study the science of the stars. One stipulation was that the observatory had to be located in a place that afforded a wide view of the night sky, without too much interference from the city's bright lights.

One day, Clark contacted a land agent and inquired as to the chances of acquiring one acre of Rothney Farm property to use for the observatory. The agent phoned back a few days later. "Good news," he said. "Mr. Cross has agreed to support the university." Clark was ecstatic. "Which acre has he decided to let us have?" he asked the agent. "You don't understand," came the reply. "Mr. Cross wants to give the university *160* acres."

Clark was floored, rendered temporarily speechless. The quarter section was assessed at $60,000 in 1970. The site proved to be perfect. "It gave us a million dollar view," says Clark. The observatory's official opening took place on January 7, 1972. The facility's 36-foot silver dome has been a shining fixture of the landscape ever since. It's one of the best teaching facilities in Canada, featuring Canada's largest telescope west of Toronto. Sandy later gave the observatory gifts of cash worth $217,500.

Just prior to the opening, Clark had a chance to meet his benefactor. Almost 30 years later, Clark offered this initial observation of Sandy: "He was just a good old prairie boy, who was interested in Alberta and its history. A very proud man, and very generous. He had a real twinkle in his eye."

Sandy came by his generosity honestly. The Cross family has a long history of giving a good chunk of its wealth back to the community, starting with patriarch A.E. Cross. He and his wife Helen, who died in 1959, were extremely giving people.

At Christmas-time in the early 1900's, A.E. would load a horse-drawn wagon with freshly killed turkeys and distribute them to neighbours for whom a Christmas turkey would have been considered a luxury item. His employees in Calgary also benefited from his generosity. The brewery was the first company in Western Canada to offer its employees a pension plan. One of A.E.'s last accomplishments in Calgary before he died in 1932 was starting a kitchen in the Stampede grounds where unemployed men were served hot porridge. As further evidence that the apple seldom falls far from the tree, the Cross children honoured their parents' memory in 1973 by donating the family home in Inglewood to the city of Calgary. The province designated it an historic resource in 1977. Today it's operated as a trendy restaurant known as The Cross House Garden Restaurant.

Calgarian Ken Carter had his first contact with Sandy, J.B. and John in 1962, when the family-owned brewery sold to Canadian Brewers. Many millions of dollars changed hands and Royal Trust — where Carter worked as a trust officer — was assigned the job of distributing the funds. At the time, Carter recalls, Sandy was "one of the boys" down at the Shamrock and National hotels. Carter notes Sandy was considered to be "the biggest rebel" among the Cross brothers because he didn't seem to have a care in the world, and took little interest in family business dealings.

Whereas John and J.B. contacted Carter regularly to ask when they could expect to receive their money from the brewery deal, Sandy showed no interest at all. Carter almost had to chase him to pay him. This could be at least partially attributed to the fact that both John and J.B. had wives and children, while Sandy was single and still living in the family house in Calgary when he wasn't staying in his cabin at Rothney Farm. The sale of the brewery, coupled with youngest brother John's purchase of Sandy and J.B.'s interest in the A7 Ranche the following year, marked the end of a long partnership among the three brothers.

Suddenly, Sandy was on his own. As the years progressed, he

Sandy Cross used to love to hear stories about the antics of wildlife such as long-tailed weasels. (Brian Wolitski photo)

spent more and more time on Rothney Farm, raising cattle and growing hay. In the process, he strengthened his connection with the land and the wildlife that relied on it. He would regularly walk the land, or tour it on horseback or in a pickup truck.

Starting in 1974, Sandy was able to share these experiences with his new wife, Ann. She accompanied him on many of his explorations of the land. Together, they talked about the past, their respective rural roots and the future.

Every now and then, Sandy would stand on the same lookout hill on which he stood in 1945, when the land evoked memories of the ranch in the Porcupine Hills where so many happy boyhood memories resided.

As he looked around in the late 1970's and early 1980's, however, Sandy began feeling a little uneasy. Expensive new homes on acreages were dotting the countryside around Rothney Farm. And the city, which once was miles and miles distant, was getting closer. The future of Rothney Farm — and the wildlife that depended on it – no longer seemed secure.

It didn't take long for Sandy to come to the realization that, before too long, he'd have to decide what to do about it.

Two great horned owls in a nest.

A mule deer doe in mid-flight in springtime.

Chapter 3
The Dream is Born

"Never doubt that a small group of thoughtful, committed citizens can change the world; indeed, it's the only thing that ever does."
Margaret Mead, world-renowned anthropologist

"I enjoyed the beautiful day yesterday. Thank you for teaching us all those new games. We loved hiking and watching those red-tailed hawks."
Mike, student, Vista Heights Elementary School

One summer evening in 1985, the telephone rang in the kitchen of Ray Glasrud's ranch house in the foothills south of Priddis. Answering it, the lanky rancher was greeted by the voice of neighbour George Crawford. A veteran lawyer with little use for small talk, Crawford got right to the point. He had a friend, Crawford explained, who wanted to do something to preserve a large tract of land long into the future. Did Ray have any ideas? Well, Glasrud certainly did have a few ideas and he was eager to share them. That brief phone call led to the creation, two years later, of the Ann and Sandy Cross Conservation Area, the largest and finest example of private land stewardship in Canada.

It was no coincidence that Crawford had chosen Glasrud as the person he'd call for advice. After all, Crawford had built a long and successful career as a lawyer, corporate director and community leader partly on his ability to know whom to call, and when. Born the son of a judge in 1915 in Edmonton, Crawford studied law at the University of Calgary and was called to the bar in 1939. He recently retired after practicing law for more than 60 years in Calgary. Crawford was a long-time partner and associate of well-known philanthropist, the late Eric L. Harvie, Q.C. In his later years, Crawford practiced as an associate with the firm of Parlee McLaws. He was named a Queen's Counsel in 1960. Crawford and his wife, Sheila, who have four grown daughters, live on a ranch along Fish Creek, just north of Glasrud's place.

Among Crawford's many accomplishments are a half-century of acting as solicitor for the Calgary Herald, and serving on the board of its parent company, Southam Inc. Crawford also was a director of Selkirk Communications Limited, Canadian Utilities Limited, Canadian Western Natural Gas Company Limited, Norwich Union, Continental Bank of Canada and the Nature Conservancy of Canada. Along the way, he somehow found time to volunteer his time in the president's chair of the Calgary Exhibition and Stampede, Y.M.C.A., Canadian Badminton Association, Alberta Light Horse Association and the Sir Winston Churchill Society. Crawford also is past chairman of the Woods Christian Home and Heritage Park, and is a fellow of the Glenbow Museum, of which he is a strong supporter. He supported and helped raise money for the

 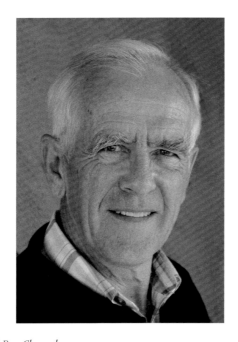 

Left to right: Motivators George Crawford, Tom Beck and Ray Glasrud.
Note: These men were later recognized as project motivators "for contributions and insight vital to the initiation" of the Conservation Area.

Canadian Guide Dogs for the Blind – taking into his home, and hunting with, Labrador retrievers deemed unsuitable as working seeing eye dogs. Crawford also worked with philanthropist Martha Cohen on building the Calgary Centre for the Performing Arts.

Crawford is a friend, lawyer and confidante of Sandy Cross. When Sandy, at age 59, married Ann Abbott in 1974, he asked George to be his best man. Crawford's phone call to Ray Glasrud that day in 1985 had resulted from a great deal of discussion between Sandy and George. For some time now, Sandy had privately confided in George his concern about the future of Rothney Farm. Sandy's concern mounted each year as an increasing number of people migrated into the country to take up residence on expensive acreages. Some lacked rural roots or any real understanding of the land for which Sandy had utmost respect. Sandy also was concerned that the city of Calgary seemed to be bursting at the seams. The city's 1985 population had topped 625,000 – more than six times larger than when Sandy started assembling his farm 40 years earlier – and it showed no signs of slowing any time soon. From the viewpoint hill on Rothney Farm, Sandy could see the city approaching his property at an alarming rate.

It bothered him that so much farmland and pastureland around Rothney Farm was being chopped up and developed into acreages. Most of these new country neighbours were nice people, Sandy thought, but he was concerned that some might not have a real appreciation for the land and for the wildlife that lived on it. Some complained about deer eating their prized begonias and ornamental shrubs, and were shocked when a coyote ate their pet dog or family cat. And if a black bear or cougar was spotted walking across their lawn, they were quick to call the game warden to try to have the creature relocated or eliminated. Many acreage owners cleared brush and trees, reducing and, in some cases, totally eliminating critical wildlife habitat just to ensure they had an open view of the Rocky Mountains.

Sandy, 71 at the time, looked around him and feared the same fate would some day befall Rothney Farm. Decades earlier, Sandy had owned some farmland in southwest Calgary, just off 14th Street south of Glenmore Reservoir. He sold it to developers and it is now part of the exclusive community of Pump Hill. Sandy didn't want the same fate to befall Rothney Farm. He worried that, when he was gone, the land would fall into the hands of developers eager to fill Calgarians' seemingly insatiable appetite for country living. The forests and brush would be cleared, the deer and coyotes squeezed out. The mere prospect of it saddened Sandy. Surely, he thought, if all this habitat and wildlife somehow could be saved, it could be used to educate school children and adults about nature, about their place in the natural order of life. If only there was a way.

Sandy and George Crawford regularly discussed business matters, to be sure, but their conversations often turned to conservation. Both men hunted game birds, and enjoyed fishing. They spent a lot of time in the field, sometimes together. George remembers Sandy, bedecked in old running shoes and blue jeans, hunting ring-necked pheasants in eastern Alberta. Sandy hunted stealthily, measuring each step and barely making a sound, his mind and body engaged in his surroundings. Both men loved talking about the animals and birds they'd seen either on their own land or in their travels, and each reveled in hearing the other's stories. "Sandy has such a feeling for the Earth, for the birds and animals," George notes. The two men were kindred spirits indeed.

One day, their conversation turned yet again to Sandy's concerns about the future of Rothney Farm. He wondered aloud if anything could be done to preserve it. George assured his old friend he'd look into it. Then he proceeded to phone neighbour Glasrud, a wildlife biologist-turned-rancher.

Born in 1947 and raised on a farm near Gravelbourg, Saskatchewan, Glasrud moved away from home to earn a bachelor of science in wildlife management at the University of Montana in 1968. Then he spent three years conducting a variety of wildlife and environmental studies for government and private agencies in the eastern Arctic, Maritime Provinces, British Columbia and New Zealand. In 1971, Glasrud joined the Canadian Wildlife Service and went north to conduct habitat surveys for various wildlife species in the Yukon and Northwest Territories. He represented the Wildlife

Service on the Yukon Interdisciplinary Land Use Team, a cooperative organization in which industry, residents and government worked together to minimize human impact on wildlife.

Glasrud left government in 1972 and signed on as environmental manager with Calgary-based Arctic Gas. He developed and implemented environmental programs for the controversial Canadian-Alaska Arctic Gas Pipeline project. Glasrud spent five years operating field programs from Alaska throughout the Yukon and Northwest Territories and into the western provinces. He maintained close contact with northern native communities, and assisted in regulatory hearings in the Yukon, NWT and the United States. He hadn't been working long in the Arctic when he started hearing about a highly respected Calgarian named Tom Beck, who had gained a strong reputation for heightening environmental and community awareness of oil companies working in the North.

In 1977, Glasrud moved to Gulf Canada Resources, where he became manager of environmental planning. Reporting to a senior vice-president, he was charged with managing environmental and community relations for several departments, developed policy and implemented a wide range of programs dealing with environmental issues, education, land use, community relations and native training. Working in close contact with government agencies across Canada, Glasrud was involved in all phases of petroleum development, including seismic, onshore and offshore drilling, gas plants, pipelines and heavy oil.

By 1982, the strapping six-foot, two-inch farm boy from Saskatchewan was ready to return to the land. He and his wife, Linda, moved to the Alberta foothills south of Priddis and started Pole Trail Investments Ltd., a farming and ranching enterprise involved in cattle, grain and hay. Glasrud contracted his expertise to government and industry in land management, drilling site construction and reclamation, wildlife management and supervision of environmental research. For the next 19 years — before he, Linda and their two children returned to Ray's roots to a ranch on the edge of the Cypress Hills in Saskatchewan — he worked hard at being a responsible steward of the habitat and wildlife on his place. He grew increasingly frustrated at the growth in rural subdivisions in his corner of the Municipal District of Foothills. "The writing is on the wall, and the writing says the city's coming, the urbanites are coming," Glasrud notes. When Glasrud first moved to the foothills in the early 1980s, he figures there were about six acreages within a four-mile radius of his place. Now there is almost 10 times that many.

According to the Municipal District of Foothills, subdivisions to create small parcels for acreages were virtually non-existent until 1968. Until then, all proposed subdivisions had to be approved first

Drops of dew on a prairie crocus.

by the Alberta government. Then the province empowered regional planning commissions to approve subdivisions, but only for four 40-acre parcels for each quarter section. Those rules were relaxed in the early 1970s, when eight 20-acre parcels were allowed per quarter. In the M.D. of Foothills, notes municipal manager Harry Riva Cambrin, a real flurry of subdivision activity occurred between 1972 and 1978, when about 1,200 twenty-acre parcels were created, mainly in the municipality's northern part near Calgary. The municipality slapped a freeze on rural subdivisions between 1980-1985, forcing landowners to take all applications to the Calgary Regional Planning Commission, then the area's overall planning authority.

Since 1985, when subdivision authority once again fell under the jurisdiction of individual municipalities, the number of acreages has jumped. Most of them have been smaller parcels of two to five acres. By the year 2000 — when a record 250 new lots were created — Foothills counted about 4,500 acreages of 20 acres and smaller. In an 11-year period between 1988 and 1999, the municipality's population almost doubled, from 9,432 to 16,122. Within the M.D., about 6,800 landowners owned 12,230 parcels of land.

Foothills council has made an effort to keep major acreage development in the northern part of the municipality – where roads and water services already exist — and off prime farmland. Riva Cambrin says there is minimal opposition to acreages in that area. Much of the opposition Foothills council receives comes from existing acreage owners who don't want to share their rural haven with newcomers. Riva Cambrin, who joined the M.D. as development officer in 1980, notes that the properties surrounding the Cross Conservation Area meet the requirements set out in the municipal development plan for land to be developed for acreages. Asked what would have happened to Rothney Farm if Sandy Cross hadn't acted on his concern for its future, Riva Cambrin is blunt: "It would have

Clematis flower.

Old paper wasps' nest on a willow.

been covered with houses."

When Glasrud received the phone call from Crawford in 1985, he couldn't help but smile. To think that a major landowner wanted to preserve his land rather than profit from it seemed a rather unique concept in this development-happy corner of the municipality. He saw potential for Sandy's protected land to become like Central Park, an 843-acre (341 hectare) public park featuring swamps, bluffs and rocky outcroppings in the center of Manhattan, New York City. Glasrud was eager to help. He recommended Crawford get together with his Arctic mentor, Tom Beck, then a member of the board of the Nature Conservancy of Canada. Glasrud offered to make the introduction.

So it came to be on a summer Sunday morning in 1985 that Beck, Crawford and Glasrud assembled on the deck at Ray's home. It was a meeting of like minds, to be sure. All three men were active outdoorsmen and committed conservationists. Crawford, Beck and Glasrud later were officially recognized as the project motivators "for contributions and insight vital to the initiation" of the Conservation Area. Years later, Sandy Cross said he believed the project wouldn't have proceeded without the trio's personal support and dedication, reinforced by their special expertise in their respective fields.

As they listened to Tom Beck talk that Sunday morning, Crawford and Glasrud were becoming increasingly excited. The more he spoke, the clearer it became that the Nature Conservancy of Canada (NCC) was the ideal answer to Sandy's concern about the future of Rothney Farm.

Launched in 1962, the NCC is a non-profit organization that takes a quiet, business-like approach to land conservation and wildlife preservation. It does this in a non-advocacy way, meaning the conservancy works co-operatively with government and the corporate sector, never openly lobbying for or against any developments that might harm or even benefit the environment. The NCC is Canada's only national charity dedicated to preserving ecologically significant areas and places of special beauty and educational interest through outright purchase, donations and conservation easements. It works by building partnerships and making creative deals with individuals, corporations, community groups, conservation organizations and government bodies that share its passion. Since 1962, the NCC and its supporters have protected 1.67 million acres across Canada.

Beck and the others had been talking on Glasrud's deck for about an hour when Sandy Cross drove up and joined them. He sat quietly in a chair, listening intently and interjecting with the occasional question, as Beck described the NCC and how it works to preserve private land. Ever the lawyer, Crawford grilled Beck for details on future land use, management and taxation issues. Glasrud recalls being impressed at that informal meeting with Sandy's "deep and abiding love of the land." When the meeting broke up, Sandy rose and smiled as he shook the hands of all three men. As he walked away, it seemed like a giant weight had been lifted from his shoulders. The seed for the Ann and Sandy Cross Conservation Area had been planted.

Beck was full of hope as he drove back to Calgary. Here was a perfect opportunity for the Nature Conservancy of Canada to establish a solid foothold in Western Canada, as earlier agreed between Beck and Dr. William Bigelow, then-chairman of the NCC. Up to then, most of its land conservation efforts had been concentrated in Central Canada, specifically in Ontario and Quebec. But Beck knew that if Sandy Cross were to get involved with the Nature Conservancy, it might just open the door for other landowners – private and corporate – in Western Canada to engage in similar arrangements to preserve ecologically-sensitive and important land. More importantly to Beck, however, was what Rothney Farm itself represented: a huge tract of prime wildlife habitat close to a major metropolitan centre that would lend itself ideally to nature education programs.

Beck certainly understood the importance of public awareness, especially when it came to environmental matters. Born in Scotland in 1932, he and his mother moved to Canada and settled in Cochrane, Alberta in 1947. His father had died four years earlier, and his mother was determined to introduce her only son to a better life in Canada.

In Scotland, Beck had grown up in the country near Wishaw. Every chance he got, he would sneak into a neighbour's private woods, where he explored the exciting natural world of hedgehogs, wild birds, blue bells and wild primrose flowers. A family friend took him fishing for trout and grayling in a nearby river, much of which was privately owned. When Beck and his mother arrived in Cochrane, the teenager was impressed by the outdoor opportunities available to everyone, not just the rich. He couldn't believe he could fish for trout in the nearby Bow River – long before

Bark designs on a poplar tree.

A group of visitors approach a stand of prairie crocus.

the river achieved its international reputation among anglers. He fished remote foothills streams, usually never seeing another person, and soon took up hunting. He honed his skills at viewing and identifying wild animals and birds, and became a committed and respected conservationist. Although his interest was keen, nobody could have foreseen then that, years later, this Scottish-born lad would become a highly significant – and understated — leader of the Canadian environmental-conservation movement.

In 1947, Beck took a job as a laboratory technician in the concrete plant at Exshaw. Then he spent 20 years with a Calgary oil company before joining the Elf-Aquitaine Group in 1970 as manager of environmental affairs. A big part of Beck's job was to work with aboriginal people affected by his company's oil and gas exploration plans in the Mackenzie Delta-Beaufort Sea region and offshore Baffin Island in the Arctic. During those years, Beck gained an appreciation for northern native people, particularly the

Inuvialuit, and strongly advocated the need to involve them in government policies and industrial development. A staunch advocate of balanced development and balanced conservation, he pioneered the concept of integrated resource planning based on environmental management and conservation principles. Beck left Elf-Acquitaine in 1980 to start a three-year stint as director of environmental and socio-cultural affairs with Petro-Canada, with operations across Canada, including the Arctic. When he left in 1983, Beck started his own Calgary-based consulting company, which he still operates.

His expertise led to many appointments to key provincial and federal boards and educational organizations, including the chairmanship of the environmental impact screening committee for Western Arctic (Inuvialuit) Claims Settlement Area in the 1990's, chairman and fellow of the Arctic Institute of North America and the chair of the Canadian Environmental Advisory Council. Beck also served as commissioner of the Mackenzie Delta-Beaufort Sea land use planning commission, and was a member of Alberta's Wildlife Management Advisory Committee. Several conservation and environmental groups also have benefited from Beck's leadership and participation, including the Canadian Council on Ecological Areas — on which he served as chairman — Canadian Nature Federation (director), and the World Wildlife Fund, where he assisted on projects. He is a fellow of the Royal Canadian

Golden Bean.

Geographic Society.

Clearly, Beck was highly qualified to judge the merit of a prospective major public conservation area within a few kilometers of Calgary. He knew that habitat loss was the biggest threat to wildlife around the world, contributing to many species becoming threatened or endangered. Rothney Farm would be one place where that would never happen. More importantly, Beck thought, was that it would be an ideal place for children from the city and elsewhere to learn about the importance of accepting nature for what it is, not for what we think it should be. And maybe, Beck hoped, this shining example of responsible land stewardship might just serve as a guiding beacon to steer other rural landowners toward similar long-term property management decisions.

In those early days, Beck was the Nature Conservancy's on-scene representative for the Cross project, handling fund-raising, making initial contacts with prospective partners and spearheading varied groundwork, including discussions with George Crawford and the Alberta government, doing media interviews, setting up and supervising a University of Calgary study and overseeing boundary surveys and brush clearing on the access road. In effect, Beck was the Conservation Area's first volunteer. (Years later, the father of five proudly saw both daughter Nancy and teenaged grandson Brady, Nancy's son, join the devoted corps of volunteers who eagerly help out in various operations of the Cross Area).

Back in the mid-1980's, Beck was on the Nature Conservancy's board when he was invited by then-chairman Bill Bigelow to take on the executive director's job. Unwilling to consider a move to the Conservancy's head office in Toronto, Beck in early 1986 instead recommended Gerry Glazier, who was working in environmental management at Petro-Canada. Beck approached Glazier and he agreed to take the assignment. Over the next two years, Glazier and Beck collaborated to firmly establish the NCC in Western Canada, in the process obtaining the first major industrial donation to the

Early Cinquefoil flower.

Low larkspur flower.

Cross Area from Chevron Canada Resources.

Following the meeting at Ray Glasrud's ranch house, Beck, on behalf of NCC, worked closely with Crawford on the deal that would lead, in 1987, to Sandy Cross donating 2,000 acres (800 hectares) of land to the people of Alberta for creation of a conservation area. With a market value of $2 million at the time, the gift was the largest private land donation in Canadian history. And that was even before Ann and Sandy donated another 2,800 acres (1,133 hectares) in 1996. Subsequent to Glazier joining the Nature Conservancy of Canada, the organization's fund-raising for the Cross Conservation Area started in earnest. Sandy Cross provided $250,000 in seed money, on a matching basis, to help fund the project.

Initially, and for the first nine years, the Nature Conservancy was charged with the responsibility of managing the area – the first property to fall under the Conservancy's direct management. A management authority, representing the public, Alberta government, M.D. of Foothills and Ann and Sandy Cross, was struck to assist the Conservancy with operations and development. The Province of Alberta was designated the official title-holder in a 99-year lease. A large part of Rothney Farm was safe at last. Beck calls the Cross Area "the most personally satisfying conservation effort of my life." Those words shouldn't be taken lightly, considering they come from a man cited for his contribution to establishment of a new national park in the Arctic and various initiatives that led to better land stewardship practices by industry.

LeRoy Fjordbotten, then Alberta's minister of Forestry, Lands and Wildlife, is a life-long cattle rancher and grain farmer on the prairies east of Granum in southern Alberta. He announced the land donation to Albertans on November 26, 1987. Fjordbotten recalls his initial reaction when he first heard through department bureaucrats that Sandy Cross planned to turn over to the province 2,000 acres of land on the condition it be preserved. "I was overwhelmed," says Fjordbotten, who resigned in 1992 after almost 15 years in politics. "That was a very generous donation, considering the proximity to Calgary and the value of that land. I've been amazed ever since at the work that's been done to preserve that legacy." The true value of the gift, says Fjordbotten, will be realized 50 years from now when the property likely will be completely surrounded by small holding developments. Stemming from Fjordbotten's initial enthusiastic involvement, the Cross Area has had continuing support from local Highwood MLA Don Tannas, various cabinet ministers – notably Gary Mar – and senior government officials who served first as members of the management authority, then on the board of the Sandy Cross Conservation Foundation.

Although Sandy's initial main focus was on preserving wildlife, he eventually insisted on three key stipulations, which formed the basis of the Conservation Area's guiding principles then and now. Listed in order of priority, the project is dedicated to:

Cow parsnip.

1. Protecting habitat and providing space for native wildlife.
2. Offering education programs, particularly to young people, without jeopardizing area wildlife and habitat.
3. Managing human use of the area through entry by appointment only.

Visitors are asked to arrange their visits at least one day in advance by phoning the automated booking line at (403) 931-9001. There is no entrance fee. To reduce drop-in traffic, the location of the conservation area is not shown on any highway signs. People who phone to arrange a visit are given directions to the site, or provided with a map. Maps also can be downloaded on the website at www.crossconservation.org.

In the early days of the Conservation Area's formation, Sandy

Cross expressed concern that the area's special nature would be spoiled and its wildlife negatively impacted if visitors were allowed to tromp unrestricted across the land. Tom Beck had proposed the rule requiring visitors to book a visit after he and his wife, Shirley, visited the world's only breeding colony of royal albatrosses at Dunedin, on the east coast of New Zealand's South Island. Tours are tightly restricted to minimize impact on the nesting giant birds.

The Conservation Area bears the names of both Sandy and Ann, who later voiced support for her husband's decision. "I think it's a good thing, I really do," she says. "It's a real gift. It should be looked after. Because I grew up in the country and lived the city life, I can see what's going on with all that beautiful country being ripped up."

True to Cross family tradition, Sandy Cross doesn't like to speak publicly about the significance or magnitude of the land donation. He appears uncomfortable when it's suggested Albertans forever will be indebted to him. Many believe that if Sandy could have donated the land without anybody knowing he was behind it, he would have happily done just that. But he and his family played such an integral role in Alberta and Canadian history — and the land donation was too significant — to permit any degree of anonymity.

When pressed, Sandy describes his donation as a natural thing to do. "I've been wondering for years what to do with the land," he notes. "This is an ideal way to preserve it." But why not just sell the

A raven perched on a fencepost watches a coyote.

farm and retire in luxury? "I don't think I'm going to starve," he says with a slight grin and a sparkle in his eye. "The almighty dollar is not everything. There's other things in life besides money."

An incredible amount of effort went into the planning and inception of the Conservation Area in 1987. But the real work was just starting. Funds had to be raised for programs and construction, and partnerships needed to be struck. Staff had to be hired, operating committees formed, trails and educational programs developed and much, much more.

So it was with little fanfare but much enthusiasm that Sandy Cross's vision was finally taking shape.

Herd of elk on a hillside at Cross Conservation Area. (Brian Wolitski photo)

Chapter 4
The Vision Becomes Reality

"I believe a chance to see wildlife under natural conditions is one of the important rights of man. It is a real enrichment of living."
Roderick Haig-Brown, noted Canadian conservationist and author

"Thank you for donating all that land, because that shows you are very generous and that you are caring for animals."
Conrad, student, McKenzie Lake Elementary School

A more fitting tribute could not have been scripted than the one Mother Nature paid to Ann and Sandy Cross on a sunny afternoon in September 1989. A crowd was gathered on a wind-swept hillside at the north end of the Ann and Sandy Cross Conservation Area for the project's official dedication. It was almost two years after Sandy Cross donated 2,000 acres of land to be preserved forever. The booming city's jagged skyline – comprised of concrete and glass monuments to economic prosperity — provided dramatic contrast against the poplar forest and Rocky Mountains that served as a spectacular natural backdrop to the podium set up on a knoll.

Speaker after speaker took to that podium to sing their praises to the Conservation Area, and to thank Ann and Sandy Cross for their generosity. Amid the formal speeches and hand shaking,

however, the true significance of the area suddenly became clear to all present. Three mule deer – two does and a young buck – ambled out of the trees and began grazing calmly on a freshly cut hayfield several hundred yards west of the podium. Eyes turned towards the deer, then people started pointing and whispering in excitement. The timing couldn't have been better. "We had a tough time tying them up out there," quipped an organizer.

Most speakers that day rambled on about vision, generosity, interpretive education and the future. But when Ann Cross strode to the microphone, she needed just fourteen words to succinctly describe the motivation behind the land donation. "We don't inherit the Earth from our grandparents. We borrow it from our children." In the audience, many people nodded their heads and responded with enthusiastic applause. And, once again, nature intervened to give veracity to the words. A red-tailed hawk drawing circles in the blue sky above the ceremony chose that moment to deliver a haunting, high-pitched cry.

One official who took the podium that day was Dick Matzke, then president of Chevron Canada Resources, which donated more than $100,000 to become one of the Conservation Area's earliest major supporters. "We are very proud to be part of the Ann and Sandy Cross Conservancy project and applaud them for their generosity," Matzke told the crowd. "Without their support, Canadians would be denied the pleasure of this beautiful oasis on

A 13-lined ground squirrel near Belvedere House.

A meadow jumping mouse hides in the understory.

the outskirts of Calgary.''

Matzke was right, of course. The project wouldn't have happened without Ann and Sandy Cross. But in the years leading up to this dedication, many other people had put their own footprint on the trail leading to the Conservation Area's transformation from vision to reality.

Even before the initial land donation in 1987, one of the required tasks was a biological inventory of Rothney Farm, to determine the exact nature of the terrain, plants and animals. The assignment went to rancher/biologist Ray Glasrud. Conducting his inventory of Rothney Farm five kilometers east of his own house, Glasrud was impressed with its ecological diversity. He classified the land as foothills parkland, a transition zone between the foothills and foothills grassland natural regions. It supports habitat from both prairie and mountain environments.

About half the area was aspen forest – with its attendant vegetation such as prairie rose, Saskatoon berry, buckbrush, pea vine and aster – while the rest was comprised of pastures of introduced grasses (42 per cent) and native prairie (eight per cent). On the area's northeast corner stand patches of rare native fescue, a common food of bison in days gone by. The fescue has had to compete to survive against brome grass, which was planted by early settlers for cattle feed. The area's major water drainage is provided by Pine Creek, which flows eastward and eventually drains into the

Children hiking.

Bow River. Glasrud was encouraged to see the area had north and south-facing slopes, plenty of natural water in springs and in Pine Creek and varied habitat. It supports animals such as mule and white-tailed deer, elk, moose, coyote, cougar, badger, long-tailed weasel, tiger salamander, beaver, muskrat, ruffed grouse, great gray owl and the highest concentration of red-tailed hawks in North America. Later inventories were conducted by students from the Faculty of Environmental Design at the University of Calgary, by the Alberta government agriculture and environment departments and by volunteer naturalists.[1]

Pat Young, Calgary-based wildlife biologist with the provincial government, notes it's unusual to have such a vast array of wildlife close to a major city. "The fact that it's a large contiguous land base that supports a lot of wildlife is highly significant," he says. Young believes it's important that young people who visit the Conservation Area are being taught about nature and conservation. It helps them

---

[1] See Appendix 1 for a complete listing of mammals, birds and plants common to the Conservation Area.

better understand the issues wildlife face, such as the need for us to maintain healthy habitat to ensure they will survive. Such lessons will stay with them for life, he believes.

In the project's formative days, the Nature Conservancy strived to ensure the local municipality – the M.D. of Foothills – and area residents understood the concept. Early in the developmental stage, Tom Beck met with Foothills council in the municipal office in High River. After hearing Beck promise the Conservation Area would be managed to the best possible standard and would strive to be a good neighbour, councillors voiced their support. Beck also acknowledged that any decisions related to developments "outside the fence" of the Conservation Area clearly fell under the M.D.'s jurisdiction and the Cross Area wouldn't interfere. Since Day One, the cooperative nature of the Conservation Area's operation is reflected in its excellent relationship with the Municipal District of Foothills. Farmer Fred Ball, then the municipality's reeve, laid the foundation for

A Swainson's hawk calling.

A great blue heron.

his council's ongoing partnership with the Cross Conservation Area by serving on the first management authority. The bond has remained strong to this day, as the M.D. council continues to appoint a member to sit on the board of the Sandy Cross Conservation Foundation.

Early organizers knew they'd earn the neighbours' support only if they were kept abreast of current and future plans. An open house was held at the Red Deer Lake community center in March 1988. Interest was high. Dozens of people showed up to view maps and other documents and to ask questions. Beck, then a trustee with the Nature Conservancy of Canada, recounts several key issues were identified, including: the threat of fire, whether cattle grazing would continue, increase in traffic flows and the fear that elk would use the area as a safe haven during the day, then invade neighbouring hay stacks and crops at night.

It was decided cattle grazing and haying would continue, both as a habitat management measure and to reduce the supply of natural fuel in the event of fire. Today, about 500 cattle graze the area yearly and 270 acres are regularly hayed. Patches of spurge and toadflax weeds are controlled by hand pulling. Thistle continues to be a weed problem that Cross Area managers are striving to control. To date, seven of the 19 springs on the Conservation Area have been revamped and protected to provide a cleaner water supply for cattle and wildlife.

Fortunately, many concerns voiced by neighbours called for solutions that the Nature Conservancy was already planning in order to satisfy two of the requirements that Sandy had laid down in the early stage: preservation of the land for habitat and wildlife in perpetuity; and controlled public access.

To satisfy neighbours' concerns and abide by Sandy's wishes, the Nature Conservancy and subsequent management have instituted several other basic rules of use: no dogs or other pets; no smoking or campfires; no camping; no horseback riding, bicycling or off-road vehicles; visitors should stay on trails and keep their distance from wildlife; no picking flowers or plants, or taking away rocks, shed antlers, bird nests etc.; no hunting or shooting; and public entry is allowed only from the main parking lot. The area is closed between 11 p.m. and 4 a.m. The operating and recreation use rules were formalized by the Alberta government, which handed down an Order-in-Council designating the Conservation Area the first Wildlife Habitat Conservation Area to be protected under the provincial Wildlife Act. The designation makes some of

From left: A house wren on a tree branch; A female mountain bluebird on barbed wire fence; A male mountain bluebird on a nest box monitored by volunteers.

the rules legally enforceable.

To the uninitiated, the rules may appear to be excessively stringent. But they reflect the true value of the gift given by Ann and Sandy Cross. The message is clear: wildlife, not people, is the top priority at the Conservation Area. The rules are needed to ensure people have the least amount of possible impact on the wild residents. That concept is key to the on-site educational program that is delivered in accordance with the wishes of Ann and Sandy.

Early in the Conservation Area's development, the Alberta government stated its firm commitment to stay atop of the elk issue. The province has tried a couple of different approaches since 1987 to reduce the elk population, including special winter-season hunts

in which hunters were allowed to use rifles to hunt elk in a broad region outside the conservation area. Traditionally, the region (outside the Cross Area, where hunting is prohibited at this time) is restricted to hunters using bows and arrows. The special rifle hunts have proven controversial. Many residents have expressed safety concerns over the use of high-powered rifles in the acreage-dotted area.

In the past several years, the province, in conjunction with the Rocky Mountain Elk Foundation and Alberta Conservation Association, has operated a 48-acre, corral-type elk enclosure on a part of the Conservation Area that's off-limits to the public. In an attempt to control their numbers in the region adjacent to the Cross

A black bear in a patch of fireweed.

White-tailed deer like this doe are commonly seen.

*The Cross Area has the highest concentration of
red-tail hawks in North America.*
(Bruce Masterman photo)

Area, hundreds of elk have been captured in the enclosure, and relocated to public lands in other parts of the province. The province is trying to maintain the area's over-wintering elk population at about 200 animals, half the number that lived in the region up to the winter of 2001. Although elk are seen as a nuisance to some, the presence of them and other wildlife helped pique the early interest of many supporters, including the Nature Conservancy of Canada.

Soon after management of the land was officially turned over to the Toronto-based Conservancy in 1987, it became apparent the agency needed a staff presence in Calgary. Up to that time, the Conservancy's interest and involvement in Western Canada had been minimal. That all changed with the largest private donation of land for conservation purposes in Canada just outside of Calgary. In May 1990, the

65

Cougar are seen occasionally. (Brian Wolitski photo)

Sightings of wildlife such as cougars and bears are prominently displayed.

NCC opened a Western regional office in Calgary.

The first employee was Alberta regional director Larry Simpson, a Calgarian with a proven track record of environmental and conservation advocacy. Suddenly, however, the oil company landman was thrust into a position that required compromise and quiet negotiation rather than open advocacy. And, no question, there was some pressure involved in overseeing development of such a massive conservation project. But Simpson proved himself worthy of the job.

Simpson fondly remembers the day, shortly after he was hired, when he made his first visit to the Conservation Area to attend a board meeting. He almost had to pinch himself as he viewed the sprawling, heavily treed property for the first time. "I was profoundly humbled to be given a role to play in this generous legacy." After his first face-to-face discussion with Sandy Cross, Simpson went away feeling even more humbled — and mightily impressed. "He has a much deeper love of the land than most people could ever understand," he adds. "Sandy looks at the land and the wildlife on it as some men might look at their children."

By the time Simpson came aboard, George Crawford, Tom Beck and the Conservancy's Gerry Glazier had already put together a management authority to operate the Cross Area. Beck, because of his involvement on the board of the Nature Conservancy, also had been directly involved in discussions with the province, particularly the Fish and Wildlife Division, fundraising, contracting for clearing and building fence lines, negotiations with the M.D. of Foothills for construction of the access road and supervision of the Strategic Management Plan team from the University of Calgary. Beck, the project's first "unofficial" volunteer, also signed up the first officially-designated volunteer, an oil industry petroleum engineer named George Funke. He contributed greatly to the initial boundary work.

When Larry Simpson joined the Nature Conservancy, his biggest and most immediate challenge was to continue a major drive already underway to raise $2 million for an endowment fund to build an interpretive building, educational program and pathways. The campaign brought together government, individuals and corporations in a show of co-operative effort seldom before seen for a conservation cause.[2]

Chevron Canada Resources was the first major corporate supporter, contributing $110,000 in the first few years after the Conservation Area was created. Chevron president Jim Baroffio and Charlie Stewart, the company's external affairs manager, offered to

Volunteers help set up a tipi each spring.

spearhead the campaign. They soon recruited Murray Todd, senior vice-president of Amoco Canada Petroleum Company Limited. In late spring of 1990, all three men joined Larry Simpson and Sandy Cross for a tour of the Conservation Area, so they could show Todd what it was all about.

Individual memories of the outing are a mix of terror and wonder. Sandy was driving a four-wheel drive vehicle that Chevron had rented for the occasion. A light snow was falling, making the trails slippery and traction difficult on steep uphill grades. Sandy persevered, his foot heavy on the gas pedal and steering wheel rotating madly as he struggled to maintain control of the skidding vehicle. His white-knuckled passengers held on for dear life.

---

[2]   See Appendix 2 for list of key early supporters.

"Mario Andretti would have been proud," recalls Simpson. Baroffio, who retired from Chevron in 1994, isn't as diplomatic: "He was undoubtedly the worst driver I ever saw. I even told him so."

Frayed nerves notwithstanding, the day was a total success. The party saw elk, deer and two red foxes. "It sold me on the whole thing and it also sold Murray Todd on getting involved," says Baroffio, who now lives near San Francisco, California. "What it boiled down to was that Sandy was so dedicated." The executives later told Sandy they'd be happy to work together to raise money to make the Conservation Area a legacy project.

Over the next eight months, Baroffio and Todd co-chaired the fundraising campaign. They worked the phone. They sent out letters to presidents and chief executive officers of major corporations, inviting them to early morning breakfast and lunch meetings to hear about the exciting project. They used various business publications to reach out for funds. "This approach to conservation is proactive and credible," Baroffio told the Daily Oil Bulletin. The Cross Area, he said, needs financial support and commitment of the private sector to "reach its full potential as a unique ecological resource." Murray Todd backed the appeal by citing the project's educational nature and opportunity for young people to be involved.

Baroffio and Todd weren't after loose change. As a starting point, they bluntly told company officials whom they met that they

Belvedere House. (Bruce Masterman photo)

needed donations of $100,000 to $200,000. Then they worked down from there. Baroffio recalls the campaign "wasn't a hard sell but it wasn't easy." It had many good selling points: the promise of outdoor education for school students, a natural area so close to Calgary, the generosity and good will reflected in the land gift and the involvement of the respected Nature Conservancy of Canada.

By May 1991, the campaign was just $450,000 shy of the $2 million goal. The Conservancy's Larry Simpson couldn't contain his joy. "I had a 14-year-old kid phone me the other day offering $1,000 which was all the money in his bank account," he told me in an interview at the time. "A retired guy walked in off the street, gave me $100 and said good luck." A few months later, the $2 million goal was reached, helped considerably by Ann and Sandy Cross's generous personal donation of $500,000. A total of 45 major donors – mainly companies, foundations and government but also private individuals – had contributed the rest. The endowment fund eventually grew to $2.3 million.

The fund was designed so that regular operating expenditures came out of the interest, not the principal. One of the first developments was an access road, provided by the provincial government with the cooperation of the M.D. of Foothills. The road was built as an extension of an existing road leading south off Highway 22X. The endowment fund paid for construction of a manager's house, at the public entrance to the area, and a stylistic low-level cedar building to house the educational, interpretive and administration operations. Generous supporter Joy Harvie Mclaren – daughter of Calgary philanthropist Eric Harvie — named Belvedere House, which is wheelchair-accessible, after a street her mother lived on in Montreal.

On October 7, 1991, the Ann and Sandy Cross Conservation Area officially opened for conservation education and limited recreation. A public open house was offered all afternoon. "The Cross Conservation Area is now Alberta's to protect and enjoy," Larry Simpson announced in a news release. Still to come was development of an extensive twenty-kilometre trail system, along with eight kilometers of interpretive paths, in addition to ambitious

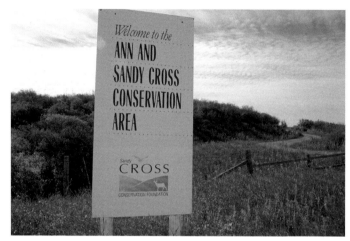

Entrance to the Conservation Area. (Bruce Masterman photo)

educational and volunteer programs. And, of course, there was staffing to arrange.

The first and only general manager to date was hired in the spring of 1992. Jacquie Gilson was pleased to be given the honour. Toronto-born Gilson was a city kid who became hooked on nature and the environment as a teenager attending summer camp in Ontario's spectacular Algonquin Park. "That solidified it for me," she says 25 years later. "I knew I wanted to work with nature and people." Gilson went on to earn degrees in geography and outdoor recreation at Lakehead University in Thunder Bay, Ontario. Moving to Calgary in 1984, she soon began realizing her career dream by working as an interpreter in Banff National Park, and then being hired by the provincial government to be the chief park interpreter in Fish Creek Provincial Park. After eight years in Fish Creek, she heard the Nature Conservancy of Canada was seeking a general manager for a major new Conservation Area near Calgary. Her application was one of many.

Gilson saw it as a fresh, exciting opportunity. It was a chance to develop an educational program for children and adults, and to help manage a very special place to celebrate the wonders of nature on the doorstep of a major metropolitan center. Before her interview, Gilson researched the project's history and the Conservancy's plans for its future. She was hired in 1992. Gilson, her husband, Neil, and their two daughters Natalie and Rebecca – then ages three years and six months, respectively – moved into the manager's residence near the Conservation Area's public entrance.

In the early days, many of Gilson's duties revolved around overseeing development of infrastructure and new programs: additional staffing, interpretive trails, wildflower gardens, educational and volunteer programs and many others. Since then, working with a small but devoted staff, Gilson has helped develop educational programs that progressively grew to involve – by the year 2000 — about 6,000 kids annually in the Chevron Cross Conservation School. Several hundred adults take

A group of children hike in front of Belvedere House.

Elk antler leans against elk interpretive sign.

continuing education workshops and conservation-related courses each year. About 1,800 people signed in to hike the area in the year 2000 — indicating the project remains a well-kept secret in a city with a population of more than 800,000. Gilson and her staff conduct an active communications program – including two newsletters and website – and a program in which people volunteer to help in several areas, including area stewardship and education. Gilson also works in conjunction with longtime Rothney Farm manager Reg Rempel to ensure the haying and cattle grazing operations are conducted properly so that they benefit the habitat. Since 1994, more than 4,000 native trees and shrubs have been planted in the Habitat Gardens around Belvedere House.

Gilson is enthusiastic when describing her involvement with the Cross Area over these many years. "It has been a phenomenal opportunity for me to be involved in such a unique and worthy project. Every day, I give thanks for the generosity of Ann and Sandy and am proud of the good that we have been able to do with it. I think the value of their gift has grown well beyond the land itself. Figuratively speaking, they provided the soil and the seeds and, by watering them, we have grown a garden of many flowers, touching many lives, with hopefully more to come."

History was made on May 5, 1993 when the first group of school kids visited the Cross Conservation Area. The event was significant on two counts: Ann and Sandy had considered environmental education so important that it was one of the area's three guiding principles; and two of Ann's grandchildren, Alexandra and Simon Abbott were among the participants. Fifty children from Nellie McClung Elementary School in southwest Calgary converged on the area on a sunny spring day. Alexandra Abbott was heard to say "It's great" as she took off with her Grades 1 and 2 schoolmates to take a "Web of Life" walk along a 3.5 kilometre trail through an aspen forest and up a grassy hill. The kids experienced several activities designed to show how various forms of nature are interconnected. They rubbed bark powder off aspen trees – the powder makes a natural sunscreen – walked like a bear, tried to jump as far as a cougar can in a single bound (six metres) and played a game that simulates elk protecting calves from predators.

Also in attendance was Tom Beck, by now a former trustee of the Nature Conservancy of Canada. "This is the culmination of the whole effort," the beaming Beck told a Calgary Herald reporter. "It makes it all worthwhile for all of us who have been involved from the beginning."

Later in 1993, Pierre Vincent, then the federal environment minister, officiated at another landmark on-site event. He presented Ann and Sandy with a coveted environmental citizenship award. "It was the couple's second major government award. In 1989, they received the prestigious Order of the Bighorn conservation award from the Alberta government "in recognition for outstanding contributions to the conservation of Alberta's fish and wildlife heritage."

In September 1996, Albertans received the surprising but welcome news that an already wonderful project had just become even better. Ann and Sandy Cross announced they were donating another 2,800 acres (1,133 hectares) to the province. The additional land was to the east and south of the original 2,000 acres (809 hectares). The project's northeast corner was just one mile (1.6 km) south of the city limits at Highway 22X. Suddenly, seemingly overnight, the Conservation Area had more than doubled in size.

The couple also donated another $450,000 in cash, to match an amount given by the provincial government and corporations. To coincide with the additional gift, management of the Conservation Area changed significantly. A newly created foundation took over day-to-day and long-term management from the Nature Conservancy of Canada. The Conservancy had managed the area since its inception in 1987. Now its role was modified to having a representative on the foundation board, along with the Crosses, local municipal officials, the provincial government and public members at large. Terms of the 99-year lease agreement with the province were amended. It expires September 19, 2095.

About 70 invited guests gathered on a sun-splashed hillside just northeast of Belvedere House for the official announcement on September 24, 1996. The mood was jubilant.

"Here we have a story of vision and a great deal of generosity," Mike Waites, president of the newly formed Sandy Cross Conservation Foundation, told the crowd. "This is a truly great treasure." Third generation rancher Roy McLean, then deputy reeve of the M.D. of Foothills, paid tribute to the couple: "Ann and Sandy Cross have bestowed a very insightful and meaningful gift to Albertans. It's not easy to speak while drooling over this grassland and natural shelterbelt. It is very important to all of us that young people have exposure to nature. They are the future stewards of the land."

Significantly, several children missed school that afternoon to be part of the celebration. Two of them – Michael Palmer and Erin Risely – were active participants in the tribute to Ann and Sandy. At the time, Michael was a 12-year-old Grade 7 student at Red Deer Lake School, a few kilometers east of the Conservation Area. Erin, then 11, was a classmate. Michael told the crowd he'd learned a lot of respect for the wildlife since his school started visiting the area in 1993. Erin said she loved birds, and always has. "I've learned about birds and migration, and about the animals that live here." The students presented the Crosses with flowers and a framed watercolour poster of the area by Calgary artist Pauline Hamill.

The day before the ceremony, Sandy and Ann met with their friend George Crawford, one of the project's motivators, and a few others in Belvedere House. As they sat at a table in the education centre where so many school kids had received lessons about the wonders of nature, they spoke about the last nine years since the first land donation was made. The couple expressed satisfaction at how the Conservation Area had been developed and utilized since 1987. "They've done a good job with this part of it so far," Sandy said. "So far, I think my wishes have been carried out. What impresses me is how (the staff) can get the attention of the kids." Ann suggested the children are the best indicators of the area's success. "Listen to the school kids. It's had some impact on them already. As far as I'm concerned, they can't be educated enough."

Sandy was asked whether his vision back in 1987 had finally been realized. He replied that he's always doubted that he ever had a vision. Muttering something about "this stuff of dreams and visions," he let the thought trail off, without finishing the sentence. Then Sandy raised his arm and pointed to a bronze plaque hanging on the wall outside the door of Belvedere House. The plaque lists the Conservation Area's guiding principles: protection of habitat and wildlife, education for young people and controlling public use. "That expresses my wishes better than any other thing," Sandy said. Enough said. End of discussion.

In 2001, the expanded Conservation Area had an estimated market value of $24 million. In anyone's books, that's a lot of money. But, for Sandy Cross, it's never been about the money. Nor will it ever be. The area's true value can never be defined in mere dollars and cents.

Red Squirrel.

A group of children sit attentively on the Aspen Trail.

Chapter 5
Nature as Classroom

"Before we can teach children, we have to give them a reason for learning; the reason being to become part of the world, thinking it together rather than in pieces."
Aldo Leopold, author of *A Sand County Almanac*

"I saw things that I have never seen before, like the skunk and the red-tailed hawk. I never knew how cool nature can be."
Jordan, student, Mountain View Academy

Educational assistant Shannon Rice shares pictures of animal tracks with her class.

Two kinds of classrooms can be found at the Ann and Sandy Cross Conservation Area.

One is inside Belvedere House, the cedar building that serves as the interpretive centre and administration office. In that classroom are displays, books and games designed to teach children and adults about nature. It's where kids can sit on small squares of carpet and listen to fascinating talks about nature. They can stand beside life-sized and painted wooden cutouts of moose, elk and deer — just to see how they compare in size. They can examine antlers and tufts of animal fur and hair. They can look at various kinds of scat in little bottles to help them identify animals living in the area by studying their droppings. They can view a model forest, and peer inside a hollow log to discover a skunk living inside. They can learn to tell the difference between mule and white-tailed deer, and why some birds fly south each fall while others don't.

In this classroom, more than 32,000 children since 1993 have learned valuable lessons about nature. By the time the students leave the traditional classroom inside Belvedere House, they are better prepared for the lessons awaiting them in the second, rather extraordinary classroom. This classroom has no blackboards, chairs, desks or books. It also lacks doors, windows and walls. But it is huge.

It encompasses 2,000 acres (809 hectares) of grasslands and aspen forests, the publicly accessible portion of the 4,800-acre (1,942 hectares) Conservation Area. It's home for the birds, animals, flowers, plants, trees and other natural components of the web of life. For those students who are willing to learn, a few short hours in this open natural classroom can teach them more about nature than they could learn in several days in a traditional classroom. The area's 8.3 kilometres of specially signed interpretive trails – two kilometres are wheelchair-accessible – are ideal for visits by school groups and other people eager to learn about nature.

That's just the way Ann and Sandy Cross always wanted it. Conservation education, particularly for young people, is considered such an important part of the Conservation Area's operation that it's listed as one of the three guiding principles. The educational component is especially important in this modern age, when many kids are raised on shopping malls and computer games, and learn about nature on the Discovery Channel. A young girl once confided in staff that she thought places like this existed only in heaven.

From top:
Volunteer naturalist Olga Droppo enjoys one of her weekly walkabouts at the Cross Area.
Volunteer naturalist Dick Choy checks a bluebird box.
Volunteer naturalist Olga shares her wisdom with school children at the pond.

General manager Jacquie Gilson noted the educational program is designed to use hands-on experience with nature games and activities to illustrate what wildlife and vegetation need to remain healthy. Every effort is made to keep learning fun and upbeat. She believes providing knowledge to school children and other youngsters will bring increased awareness and an enhanced sense of environmental stewardship that could stay with them for the rest of their lives. And that, according to Gilson, has the potential to be extremely beneficial to the environment in the long term. "You won't protect what you don't understand or appreciate," she said. Gilson knows the benefit of educational field trips first-hand as it was a school trip to a conservation area in Southern Ontario which got her interested in the outdoors. "Who knows what future good these students will be able to do for the environment?" she wonders.

***

A core component of the educational program is the Chevron Cross Conservation School. It's named after Calgary-based Chevron Canada Resources, which has been a major financial supporter of the Cross Area since the beginning. In addition to educational materials and staff support, the company generously provides subsidized bus transportation to the Area for classes from high-needs schools in Calgary. The school offers five innovative and exciting programs aimed at students in Grades 1 to 9. All programs are designed to teach young people about the environment and conservation. They're increasingly popular with teachers, because of the excellent leadership provided by area staff and volunteers, and the fact the kids are actively engaged while learning. Most of the subjects couldn't be taught properly in an urban school setting.

On a Friday afternoon in spring 2001, Chevron president Jim Simpson left the hectic pace of his 23rd floor office in downtown Calgary to make his first visit to the Cross Area. Although several preceding Chevron presidents had been out there in

Students walking in line.

Educational assistant Shannon Rice holds a finger to her mouth to get the students to be quiet.

years past, Simpson hadn't had a chance since his recent appointment and transfer to Calgary. But within minutes of setting out on a hike with general manager Jacquie Gilson and Tom Beck, vice-president of the Sandy Cross Conservation Foundation, Simpson was quietly vowing to return soon. He spied six mule deer as they wandered, calmly in single-file, away from a dugout into the trees. It was early afternoon; the deer shouldn't have been active that early in the day, but perhaps the heat had forced them into an afternoon drink of water. Their motivation didn't really matter. It's always a thrill to see wild deer within minutes of city limits. For Simpson and the others, seeing them just a few hundred metres away was a real bonus.

A few minutes later, Simpson stopped to greet a school group returning from a guided hike. "What have you seen?" he asked the youngsters. Unaware they were speaking to the head of a company that made possible their visit, the youngsters enthusiastically regaled Simpson with stories. They'd been to the pond and spotted an insect – likely a backswimmer – swimming with "arms like

From top:
Susan Hayduk: education and volunteer program manager.
Chevron Canada Resources president Jim Simpson speaks to school children during a hike on the Cross Conservation Area.
Chevron president Jim Simpson and Jacquie Gilson, Cross Area general manager, approach a sun-bleached elk antler that had been naturally shed by a bull elk a few years earlier.

paddles." They'd hiked through a beautiful valley. They told Simpson about the mule deer near the dugout, and seemed pleased that he'd seen them too.

Later, Simpson expressed amazement at the students' boundless enthusiasm. "It was incredible just to see the joy on their faces," he said. "It's so different than a formal classroom situation. What a great way to learn."

Simpson said Chevron is proud to be part of the Cross Area. He noted the oil industry, in which Chevron is a key player, can't help but have an impact on the environment just by the very nature of the business. Supporting the Conservation Area is one way his company can offset that impact, Simpson added.

There's no question Chevron has made a huge contribution toward shaping the environmental consciences of young minds through its generous support of the Cross school programs from the start. The description of the five core programs may differ, but they share a common theme: responsible environmental stewardship.

For example, in the Winter Walkabout program, students in Grades 1-2 become deputy rangers and investigate winter. They study animal tracks and signs, learn that snow is an excellent natural insulator and discover how plants survive the winter. The Amazing Mini Adventure, for Grades 2 and 3, shows students how to investigate the miniature world of insects, spiders and other bugs in three different habitats.

The Web of Life allows Grades 3-5 students to walk along the 3.5 kilometre Chevron Aspen Trail to see the forest through the eyes of a spider – figuratively-speaking, of course – in order to discover the important role each species plays. Keepers of the Land, for Grade 4 students, challenges students to experience land as a natural resource. Grade 6 students take the Forest Explore program to study the aspen parkland while making nature observations, practicing plant identification and learning about forest ecology.

School children gather for a hike.

Educational assistant Shannon Rice (left) and volunteer Catherine Southwood do an orientation session for students in Belvedere House.

In 2000, the Conservation Area piloted an Open Minds school, also sponsored by Chevron. In this program, school children visit the area every day for one week, rather than the usual one-day visit. Staff members have developed various programs for groups such as Girl Guides and Boy Scouts. These badge-related programs provide youth with conservation education opportunities outside of school hours. Summer day camps for six to 12 year olds are popular with rural and urban audiences. The children spend a week on-site exploring nature and having fun while on "Safari."

Susan Hayduk, education and volunteer program manager, is directly responsible for the Open Minds Program. She believes it has great potential, since one week of learning is better than just one day. "The Open Minds program awakens a 'natural intelligence' in kids," Hayduk says. "By the end of their week, they understand how they are connected to nature and why wilderness is important."

Hayduk notes a typical week usually takes kids through a wide range of awareness. The first day, the children are in awe of the beauty and vastness of the Conservation Area. By the second day, they have established a special spot they visit each day. It is here that they begin to hone their observation skills. On the third day, the sea of green they faced on Day One has become a familiar world of distinct colors, textures and purposes. They have now taken ownership of the Area, and their questions turn into a detailed analysis of what they experience. On the fourth day, Hayduk says, the children's senses are at their peak and their journals reflect a connection to nature's spirit. The fifth and final day is a quiet time filled with positive reflection, and one last chance to visit their favorite place. The kids also feel some sadness on this day, because they know they are leaving. After the last day, their

A young student uses binoculars to get a close-up view.

Chayse Monty, aged six, is eager to answer a question while his Stephanie, looks on.

teachers will continue to build on their experience back at school. And the children will now be able to go out into the world knowing their special connection to nature and the importance of wilderness.

The children themselves are best qualified to pass judgment on the programs. And they eagerly do just that, in written letters or drawings depicting what they learned on their visits. Letters are hand-written (or scrawled) in lead, ink, crayon and colored markers. Most are adorned with pictures of flowers, animals, trees and buildings. A sampling of comments made by kids in recent years is revealing:

"Without you I would have never known about this."

"I think your nature school is a blast."

"Thank you for providing all that land. I really appreciate it. You guys are great."

"I learned a new word for poop."

"We had fun looking for the tracks and animals."

"I learned not to pick the flowers."

"Thank you for the wonderful tour. It was 2,000 thumbs up."

***

It was a crisp October morning when 24 exuberant Grade 6 students from Calgary stampeded off a yellow school bus in the parking lot just north of Belvedere House. After strapping on backpacks, they walked along the gravel road up the hill to the interpretive centre. Volunteer leader Catherine Southwood welcomed the students and started their orientation. After telling them about the land donation by Ann and Sandy Cross, she asked them whose place it was now, evoking shouted answers of "the animals" and "the bears." Southwood told them it was important to stay on the trails when they went on their hike, and asked if the kids knew why. A young girl shouted out, "So you don't get lost." Another girl responded, "So you don't scare the animals away." Catherine explained that it's easier on the wildlife habitat if people don't trample or scatter litter on it. Major ground rules established, the group exited Belvedere House and entered the larger, natural classroom.

As the sun peeked through the dark clouds, the students were introduced to education assistant Shannon Rice, a 23-year-old graduate of the environmental conservation program at the University of Alberta. The soft-spoken young woman had to wait several seconds until the students became quiet enough for her to speak. "I know you're all excited about seeing all kinds of animals and deer and bears but you probably won't," she said, noting the group likely will make too much noise to see much wildlife. But they proved her wrong as, suddenly, one of the kids spotted a little black beetle scrambling across the gravel path. A minute later, the group stopped at a mound of dirt with a hole in it. Rice explained it was a den of a rodent commonly known as a gopher, but that's actually a Richardson's ground squirrel. Further along the path, the group encountered low mounds of dirt in a crooked line. Pocket gophers – a true gopher – had been digging underground tunnels.

The field trip continued west along a forest trail blanketed with fallen yellow and brown leaves. Under Rice's supervision, the students put leaves between pieces of cardboard and onionskin paper, and rubbed with a crayon to make a leaf picture. Rice explained how the powder on the bark of an aspen tree makes effective natural sunscreen. The group stopped to look at a patch of moss at the base of a poplar tree. With moss growing on one side of the tree but not the other, Rice prodded, which way is north? "That way! That way!" a chorus of young voices eagerly replied while arms pointed in every possible direction. Smiling, Rice pointed north towards Highway 22X. "It's *that* way," she said.

Throughout the hike, Rice engaged the kids in easy, informative banter that encouraged their participation. She asked them what they thought of bears. The responses ranged from "They're cool" to "They're scary". Rice pointed out there's no need to be scared of bears. But she urged the students to respect them by making noise in bear country to avoid surprising them, and staying clear of sow bears with cubs. Rice described how the students could move like a bear. Separating the kids into groups, she urged them to appoint one person to be the bear's head, another the body, and four to be the legs. The result was a great deal of awkward contortions and stumbling along the path.

Rice talked about red foxes, about the need for them to have keen senses of smell – "they can smell better with wet noses" – and hearing because most of their hunting is done under dark of night. The group followed the trail out of the trees and onto the edge of a grassy hillside before stopping to inspect dozens of small dried-out brown pellets scattered in the grass. "Does anybody know what that is?" Rice asked. Several crude answers followed, but not the correct one: elk scat. She recited a simple field guide to deer family scat identification: "Deer are like chocolate-covered raisins, elk are like chocolate-covered peanuts and moose are like chocolate-covered almonds."

On a lunch break on the hillside Rice discussed the enjoyment she gets from teaching nature to young people. Most children, especially urbanites who haven't been exposed to the outdoors, see nature in a different light than those who have, she said. Growing up in Edmonton, Rice became interested in the outdoors while fishing with her father. She watched every televised nature show she could find, and decided to make nature a career.

Upon their return to Belvedere House, the kids were getting loud and fidgety in anticipation of the bus trip home. Rice, however, was determined to complete the program with a serious wrap-up message. "The most important thing you can remember is that everything in the forest depends on everything else," she said. "For

Top: A student examines elk antlers on a shelf in Belvedere House. Below: Tom Beck (left, pointing), Chevron president Jim Simpson and Jacquie Gilson, Cross Area general manager, during a hike on the Conservation Area.

example, you have butterflies that help pollinate flowers. If all the butterflies die, then how will the flowers get pollinated? Everything has a part in the web of life. If you take away a part, you destroy the web."

Shannon Rice's commitment is representative of the staff at the Cross Area. Employees choose to work there not because it's a job, but because they believe in conservation. They wish to do their part to help educate the masses in the pragmatic, yet often mysterious, ways of nature. An understanding of nature – both academic and practical – and a strong personal interest in spreading the message reinforce the employees' enthusiasm. It's a sure-fire recipe for a successful nature education program.

***

A similar quality can be found in the volunteer program. General manager Gilson refers to volunteers as the lifeblood of the Cross Area. In the year 2000, 76 people contributed almost 3,900 hours of volunteer service in all aspects of the operation. The average volunteer commitment was 44 hours a year. Some volunteers serve as area stewards – Susan Hayduk, volunteer manager, calls them the area's eyes and ears – who head out on regular hikes to record wildlife sightings, habitat concerns or evidence of improper use. They also help out in conservation education, communications, special events, open houses and various presentations.

The role of volunteers is important. With only a handful of paid staff, it would be otherwise impossible to assign an employee to each hiking group or educational program that requires leadership. Clearly, there's a general recognition of the importance of dispensing accurate information, and not having newcomers go home with the wrong perception of any aspect of the operation. Volunteers receive special training, to ensure they know the history of the area and understand what it's all about. New volunteers regularly receive training from other knowledgeable volunteers such as Olga Droppo.

A Calgary naturalist and author of *A Field Guide to Alberta Berries* (1987), Droppo first hiked the area in the late 1980's. She was impressed with the diversity of the terrain, varied wildlife and rich plant life. Ever since, she has been involved in the Conservation Area in some way, including planting wildflowers and shrubs, guiding hikes and volunteering as a steward. Over the years, Droppo has recorded more than 300 plant species – and their Latin names – that are found here. She's also helped identify 26 mammal species and more than 100 different birds. Few people can match Droppo for her knowledge of the area's flora and fauna. "She's a very good teacher," said Dick Choy, a naturalist and volunteer who's learned much from Droppo since he first visited the Cross Area in 1997.

In early spring 2001, Droppo embarked on one of her regular Wednesday morning "walkabouts" to check the season's progress. Spring, late season rather than early, is her favorite time at the Cross Area. That's when plants and flowers are in full bloom, or not far from it, and leaves have formed on trees and willows. On that day in late April, however, not much new growth was happening. Remnants of a late snowfall lay heavy in the trees and on the trails on north-facing hillsides. Droppo was using a walking stick. When you're 70 and waging what's already been a 50-year bout with diabetes, any kind of hiking aid is welcome, especially when snow covers the trail.

Walking down a hill south of Belvedere House, Droppo carefully scanned the trees and fields for any sign of life — plant or wildlife. Although she's hiked the area hundreds of times, she never tires of it. No two hikes are ever the same. She is forever noticing something new, perhaps a fresh green sprout of a plant in spring, or a previously unseen bird nest that suddenly became visible after leaves dropped in late autumn. Once, she heard the repeated hoot of a barred owl during a lunch stop near the Stewart Barn. One trip she might notice a single prairie crocus poking up through the snow. The next week, Droppo will visit the same location and marvel to see dozens of those fuzzy mauve harbingers of spring. "This area is always changing, not just by season but day-by-day," she said.

She stopped walking, planted her walking stick in the snow and pointed at a delicate trail of tiny padded tracks dimpling the snow. "A meadow vole," Droppo observed. "It should be careful crossing an opening like this considering the number of owls living here." Suddenly, a tiny flash of brilliant blue seemed to light up a grassy clearing six metres away. Another blue flash. Then, it too was gone in a wink. It appeared the pair of mountain bluebirds was too busy to tarry; perhaps they had a nest to tend.

That wasn't the only natural treat in store for her that day. Further along the trail, she spotted a white patch in the trees. When she stopped, the patch turned into the back end of a mule deer. Droppo watched as 12 deer bounded out of the safety of the trees and into an open field. Obviously nervous at being so exposed, they quickly moved across the opening, and then seemed to relax as they entered another stand of poplars. Slowly, they worked their way through the trees toward the foot of a ridge. Seconds later, they had disappeared — leaving their tracks in the snow and another special springtime memory for Olga Droppo.

***

Sandy Cross used to worry that some city people who moved to expensive acreages weren't adequately prepared to accept all the realities of country living. Now, thanks to the Conservation Area that he created, there's no excuse.

The year 1999 marked the start of the highly successful Conservation Matters series of information sessions. The program, part of the foundation's Beyond the Boundaries initiative, is designed to provide local people with relevant and timely information on important conservation topics ranging from predators and weed control to land stewardship and wildlife corridors.

The program is especially beneficial to new rural residents, people who might not have fully understood what they were getting into when they moved from the big city into the country.

That was clearly the case for many people who attended a session on cougars one winter night at Belvedere House. Biologist Martin Jalkotzky spoke of the best cougar habitat in North America being in the foothills southwest of Calgary. Even better — at least from the cougars' standpoint — many acreage owners tend to keep goats, sheep and other domestic animals that are "like Big Macs to every predator worth his salt." Jalkotzky pointed out that the increase in acreages in the northwest corner of the M.D. of Foothills was putting even more pressure on cougars. Around the packed room, many people shook their heads, their eyes wide in disbelief.

When Jalkotzky invited questions, a woman tentatively raised

Children look through a telescope on Star Night, an evening educational program in which people learn about the solar system.

her hand and asked, "Are there cougars, like, right here?" The answer is a definitive yes. Cougars indeed have been spotted on the Conservation Area over the years, and several sightings and acts of predation – on pet dogs, cats, goats and sheep – are reported annually on nearby foothills properties. Jalkotzky urged residents to respect the needs of cougars and accept that they live in the area. Keep pets and small domestic animals safely locked up at night, he suggested, adding that acreage owners should also clear vegetation around their houses and not let children play unsupervised in the woods. If a cougar should attack, Jalkotzky said, you should fight back. "But the likelihood of a cougar attacking is a whole lot less than getting in your car and getting smacked on Highway 22X," he added.

Concern over bears, primarily black bears, was raised at another Conservation Matters seminar. Researcher Karen Oldershaw, who worked on the Eastern Slopes Grizzly Bear Project, told residents that people moving to the foothills near Calgary must understand they're heading into an ecologically rich area with many wildlife species, including bears. "Game wardens are often called by people who are outraged that nobody told them bears lived there also," she said. Oldershaw recommended rural residents remove from their properties any items that might attract bears, including bird feeders and horse food. Gardens are "easy pickings" for bears unless they're surrounded by an electric fence, she advised. Black bears are attracted by berry bushes and such unlikely

Educational assistant Shannon Rice shows children how to make animal tracks in winter.

substances as anti-freeze and motor oil that's spilled on a driveway. Once again, many people in the audience were surprised to hear that their neighbours included bears.

Part of the Cross Area's educational component isn't as visible. For example, the area offers an excellent opportunity for university and other post-secondary school students to conduct basic and applied research on such subjects as geology, biology and environmental science. This important role dates back to 1988, when students from the Faculty of Environmental Design at the University of Calgary prepared the Conservation Area's first management plan. University students from Calgary and Edmonton have studied wildlife movement patterns and restoration of native prairie.

In recent years, the Ann and Sandy Cross Conservation Area has reached out to the community to offer continuing education programs for families, adults and children. Topics have included birds, wildflowers, nature photography, animal tracks and signs, elk, the solar system, insects and ecology. The programs have proven to be very popular.

The reasons are twofold: area residents have come to view the area as a spectacular natural classroom, and much of what's being taught isn't available anywhere else.

One of the most popular programs was a winter session called Winter Tracks, presented in January 2001. Eight kids, ages six to 10, and their parents showed up at Belvedere House to learn. For the next few hours, the youngsters discovered – with games and other activities – how wildlife copes in winter. They put gelatin in plastic film canisters and called them "mice." Then the kids buried them in the snow and retrieved them more than an hour later. The gelatin wasn't frozen; the "mice" had survived. The reason? Snow is a natural insulator and wildlife such as mice has learned to survive sub-zero temperatures by burying themselves in it. If snow weren't such an excellent insulator, bears tucked away for their prolonged sleep each winter would freeze solid.

The youngsters also learned how to make plaster casts of tracks, and to identify different wildlife by the tracks they make in the snow. They were told a snowshoe hare turns white in winter, all the better to hide from predators such as foxes, cougars and coyotes. And weasels turn white so they can sneak up on mice and other tasty meals.

For mother Stephanie Monty, the session was a perfect opportunity for her son, Chayse, then six, to pursue his interest in wildlife. They'd recently moved to the Priddis area after four years in Calgary. Before that, the family lived in Windsor, Ontario, where Stephanie said there "aren't many open spaces like this, but there is lots of pollution." She said Chayse loves to hear coyotes howling at night and watch a skunk that lives behind their house. The Conservation Area, Stephanie Monty said, is a perfect place to teach him more about the wild things he loves.

Jayce Wilson, nine, and his mother, Sharon, drove from their ranch near Black Diamond to participate. The youngster has already shown a keen interest in fishing, hiking, camping, horseback riding and hunting. But Sharon was interested in providing him with more information about wildlife and conservation, especially the need to preserve habitat so wildlife will thrive. They'd previously attended sessions on bugs, owls, elk bugling in autumn and stars. "Jayce goes to these things, then goes to school and tells all his friends about them," Sharon Wilson said. "We learn stuff that I didn't even know about. We're certainly learning a lot more this way." And what did Jayce think? "Most of this stuff I already know," he replied, as only a confident nine-year-old boy could.

Not all the lessons taught at the Conservation Area are of this world. Take, for example, Star Night. About 70 kids and their parents showed up outside Belvedere House on a Wednesday evening to learn about the solar system. Later, when it grew dark, they huddled outside and peered at the stars and the moon through powerful telescopes set up on the back lawn. When the evening's program started, a strong west wind buffeted the crowd as general manager Jacquie Gilson placed a Nerf ball on the ground near Belvedere House. The ball represented the Sun. Using grains of sand and small pebbles to represent the various planets, she methodically counted off steps to mark the relative distance between each one. The crowd kept in step with her. Some kids ran ahead to be first to reach the next "planet." Finally, all the planets in relation to the Sun were marked off on the gravel trail: Mercury, Venus, Earth, Mars, Jupiter, Saturn, Uranus, Neptune and finally Pluto, the farthest away from the Sun. "How does Pluto feel?" Gilson asked the crowd. "Cold!" shouted several voices, young and old.

"Who thinks there is life out there in other solar systems?" Gilson asked.

More than a dozen hands shot up. Several people muttered, "I do."

"I do, too," Gilson replied. "But as far as we know, Earth is the only place in our solar system with life." The crowd grew silent as she continued.

"I'm glad we have the solar system, so we can have Earth so we can have the Cross Area."

Seventy-five heads nodded as one. They seemed to be saying amen, which would have been rather fitting.

A small tree grows on a sandstone formation.

Kassidy Hiebert, Belvedere Parkway School.

Alexis (Lexi) Handford, Glen Meadows School.

Melisse Horne, Belvedere Parkway School.

Tyler Maggrah, Belvedere Parkway School.

Kelsi Rasmuson, Eugene Coste School.

Cristy Carlson, McKenzie Lake School.

Breanna Lee Vandermeer, A.E. Bowers School.

Alicia McCance, McKenzie Lake School.

Colby Lowten, A.E. Bowers School.

Kayla Kinnear, Belvedere Parkway School.

Catharine Kavanagh, Our Lady of Peace School.

Megan Teminsky, Glen Meadows School.

Courtney Gray, A.E. Bowers School.

Kayla Hungle, Eugene Coste School

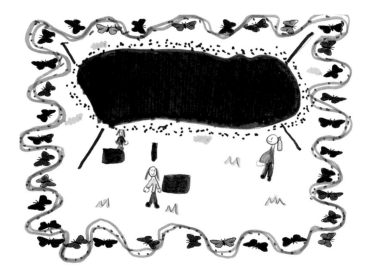

Emily Hughes, Our Lady of Peace School.

Sebastian Soto-Erica, Glen Meadows School

A stand of prairie crocus.

Chapter 6
The Land Preservation Movement

"The task is urgent. The potential that still exists is being lost as endangered spaces are being swallowed by our thoughtless devotion to development at any cost."
Ian McTaggart-Cowan, internationally-recognized conservationist, dean emeritus (graduate studies), professor of zoology, University of British Columbia

"I liked it when we went to the forest. I learned that I shouldn't squish ants and other bugs. I liked the Cross Conservancy."
Madyson, student, Our Lady of Peace Elementary-Junior High School

The stewardship legacy of the Ann and Sandy Cross Conservation Area has rippled across Canada like a pebble landing in a pond. The couple's gift of 4,800 acres (1,942 hectares) of private land is the largest piece of property ever donated for conservation purposes in this country, and is among the largest in North America. The project's significance is further enhanced by its location — on the doorstep of a prosperous metropolis with a population expected to top one million within the next decade — and its diversity of terrain and wildlife. Monte Hummel, president of the Toronto-based World Wildlife Fund Canada, calls the Cross area "an outstanding precedent for private land stewardship which is recognized and well regarded beyond Alberta, right across Canada." Ann and Sandy Cross "set an inspiring example for others to voluntarily commit land to its highest purpose, namely long term conservation."

It's impossible to pinpoint exactly how many private landowners in Canada have been motivated by the Cross donation to act now to preserve their ecologically sensitive property well into the future. But there's no question the Cross Conservation Area has been a catalyst in the land preservation movement in Alberta and across Canada. In Alberta, the creation in the late 1990's of the Southern Alberta Land Trust Society — dedicated to preserving rangeland in southwestern Alberta — was inspired at least in part by the success of the Cross project. The Cross land donation also prompted the Nature Conservancy of Canada — at Tom Beck's urging — to expand into Western Canada with an office in Calgary. The move was significant both to the NCC and to the land preservation movement in general, because it increased the organization's area of interest into Alberta, Saskatchewan and Manitoba. Between its creation in 1962 and 1990, the Conservancy had protected 80,000 acres across Canada. Since 1990, when the Calgary office opened, that total has increased to about 1.7 million acres.

The movement to preserve private land has gained momentum across the country in the past decade, and especially in the last five

years. The beneficiaries are many, including: the land itself, the wildlife and vegetation that rely on the land, local residents and other Canadians who care about nature. There's also a significant economic benefit. A 1996 federal government study on the importance of wildlife to Canadians showed nature-related activities – many of them on private land – contribute $11 billion annually to the Canadian economy, with $1.2 billion in Alberta alone. Some people believe nature is too *special* to put a price on it. However, the general consensus among conservation leaders is the special-ness of nature is exactly why a dollar value should be attached to it. The pure and simple truth is that economic worth speaks louder than intrinsic aesthetic values in corporate and political arenas, where most decisions impacting nature are made. And, if that weren't enough, nature provides additional economic benefits in the industries of agriculture, forestry and fishing, which account for 13.6 per cent of the Gross Domestic Product and employ 2.3 million Canadians. Like it or not, nature is big business.

There's no question nature needs all the help it can get in Canada right now. More than 300 species are classified at risk, which means they're classified as endangered, threatened or of special concern – there's a chance they'll become threatened or endangered if nothing is done to help them now. Loss of habitat – much of it on private land – is the major cause. Contributing to that reduction is population growth – with its inherent double-whammy of urban development and resource-based industries such as mining and forestry. The problem is aggravated

Top: Hiker rests on a sandstone formation. (Bruce Masterman photo)
Centre: David Anderson, federal environment minister, and Jacquie Gilson, Cross Area general manager, tour the Conservation Area in May 2001.
Bottom: Guy Greenaway, of Southern Alberta Land Trust Society, and Jacquie Gilson, Cross Area general manager, speak at a Conservation Matters meeting in Belvedere House.

when you add other factors into the mix: air and water pollution, climate change and ozone depletion, excessive harvesting of plant and animal species, consumption and production patterns such as single-crop farming, and invasive, non-native species such as purple loosestrife and zebra mussels. By protecting nature, Canadians are protecting the quality of life of future generations. As one walks in areas preserved with love and vision — such as the Cross Conservation Area — it is difficult to contemplate life without wild birds, animals, reptiles, plants, wildflowers, trees – all ingredients that contribute to a rich and full life for all people. The responsibility for protecting nature is not a task that can, or should, be left only to governments. It's a grassroots issue. If nature is to survive, all Canadians must do their share.

Fortunately, millions do just that. They belong to naturalist and conservation organizations – such as Ducks Unlimited Canada, Trout Unlimited Canada, World Wildlife Fund, Rocky Mountain Elk Foundation and Nature Conservancy of Canada — where they learn about flora and fauna, and the many issues facing nature. They volunteer for on-the-ground projects designed to help wildlife through habitat development and other projects. They attend fundraising banquets and make special donations to these organizations and others. Ducks Unlimited Canada pioneered the concept of working with private landowners for habitat protection and improvement in this country. It has secured almost 19 million acres of wetlands habitat – and developed 5,700 habitat projects — since it was founded in 1938. By the year 2000, DUC had spent almost $993 million on conservation work, much of it on the Prairie Provinces through the North American Waterfowl Management Plan, a groundbreaking continental program supported by Canada, the U.S. and Mexico.

Canadians also help by encouraging and facilitating school and community nature programs for youth — priming the pump so to speak — to create responsible future stewards of the land. Much can be done for wildlife in our everyday lives. Domestic pets can be kept under control – dogs leashed in natural areas and cats belled in urban centers – to reduce their impact on wildlife. Drivers can slow down in areas where wildlife is found. Trees, shrubs and wildflowers can be planted to provide habitat; conversely, existing vegetation used by wildlife can be maintained and enhanced. You can buy food grown without harmful herbicides and pesticides, and other so-called "green" goods such as eco-certified lumber and papers. Recycle plastic products and avoid disposable plastic packaging, which can be deadly to birds and animals. You can avoid littering and putting toxic substances down storm sewers, where they'll end up in rivers and lakes. Boaters can take care not to spill oil and gas into the water, and avoid traveling in shallow areas which are critical habitat for spawning fish, nesting birds and aquatic plants and invertebrates. You can support various provincial and federal habitat conservation programs. Landowners also can choose to preserve their land — as Ann and Sandy Cross did — through measures such as conservation easements, ecological gifts and other agreements.

Land preservation and responsible stewardship are two of the most effective tools available to Canadians wishing to counter the threat posed by habitat destruction. Monte Hummel, who has been involved in national environmental and conservation issues for more than three decades, says long-term land conservation is much more than a "nice thing to do." Rather, he and others in the front lines of the land stewardship movement believe it is a critical component to rounding out a representative system of protected areas, complementing parks, wilderness areas and ecological reserves on public land. More than half of Canada's most critical wildlife habitat is on private land. Private stewardship of that land helps bring back endangered species. It also ensures that working landscapes — land that may still be grazed or logged in a sustainable manner — are used in ways that respect the biological integrity of the land. Hummel is encouraged that educational programs offered to school children and other young people at the Cross Area are helping to reinforce that important message. After all, students of today are the landowners, corporate leaders and voters of tomorrow. It's important to open their eyes now to critical issues because — unfortunately — the issues will probably still be there when they grow up.

It is illuminating that Sandy Cross, whose ties to the property on which the Conservation Area is located date back to 1945, never refers to Rothney Farm as *my* property, or *my* land. He always, respectfully, calls it *the* land. Private land stewardship provides the opportunity for landowners to honour a principle touted many decades ago by Aldo Leopold, widely regarded as the father of modern-day conservation: "A thing is right when it tends to preserve the integrity, stability and beauty of the biotic community. It is wrong when it tends otherwise." Under Leopold's criteria, the Ann and Sandy Cross Conservation Area and projects like it are very right things indeed.

"This spot is a perfect example of the kind of conservation leadership individual Canadians are showing all over the country," said David Anderson, Canada's environment minister, during a speech at the Conservation Area on May 3, 2001. "It is especially fitting that we are here today, in an area dedicated to protecting habitat and providing space for native wildlife." Anderson was there to announce $700,000 in federal funding for conservation

Spring comes to the forest as a fringe of green appears behind a stand of aspen trees.

stewardship projects in Alberta. After his speech, Anderson went for a short tour of the area with general manager Jacquie Gilson. As if on cue, two herds of deer appeared in a nearby field, just as they tend to do on special occasions. Their appearance was like an exclamation mark to Anderson's speech.

Responsible stewardship of private land in Canada is becoming increasingly critical to the future of wildlife. Quite simply, not much remaining undesignated public land lends itself to creation of new parks. Much of the remaining public land that isn't already covered by some sort of legislative protection is subject to many historical uses – including grazing, mining, logging and oil and gas development – which would pose too many political and practical hurdles to stop or alter in any way. This is especially true in Canada's southern region. "Government has run out of gas as to its ability to create new parks," notes Clayton Rubec, chief of habitat conservation with the Canadian Wildlife Service. "We have to recognize that creating parks for wildlife isn't the only way of doing business." Government-supported programs in which landowners preserve their land through mechanisms such as conservation easements and ecological gifts are better suited to the modern situation.

Since 1995, Canadians have donated more than 200 gifts of land – covering more than 44,000 acres (18,000 hectares) and valued at more than $28 million – under a new ecological gifts program managed by Environment Canada. Canadian landowners donated hundreds of land parcels under other rules prior to 1995. That year, however, marked the start of a special federal program that significantly enhanced tax breaks for landowners donating ecologically sensitive land, easements and covenants. The changes followed heavy lobbying by organizations such as the Nature Conservancy of Canada, The North American Wetlands Conservation Council and the National Round Table on the Environment and the Economy. Gifts can include full title to a property, or the value of a conservation easement, covenant or servitude as defined by provincial or territorial legislation. Land can be donated outright or the landowner can choose to keep it, but with restricted long-term use or perhaps limited access.

Gifts donated so far include: cliff, beach and coastal wetland habitats in New Brunswick; waterfront wetlands and woodland properties in Ontario; foothill and mixed boreal woodlands in Alberta; grassland habitats in Alberta and Saskatchewan; and oceanfront forest and desert steppe areas in British Columbia. [3]

Under the program, individuals or corporations can donate private land to federal, provincial or territorial governments, Canadian municipalities or one of 136 federally approved

---

[3]   See Appendix 3 for list of contact agencies, organizations and
      further references.

A great gray owl peeks around a poplar tree.

charitable organizations across the country. In return, individuals receive a federal tax credit and corporations get a deduction for the fair market value of the donated land. The credit or deduction amounts to 17 per cent of the first $200 of the land value, and 29 per cent of the remaining. Further benefits accrue through reduced federal surtaxes and provincial taxes. These credits and deductions – unlike other charitable donations – can be used against up to 100 per cent of the donor's annual income. Unused portions of the tax credit or deduction can be carried forward for up to five additional years. The Income Tax Act was further amended in February 2000 to reduce by 50 per cent the amount that would otherwise be included as income on any capital gains associated with the gift.

In the spring of 2000, the federal government announced new funding — $45 million over five years — for a new habitat stewardship program aimed at species that are at risk (endangered, threatened or of special concern), or for species for whom stewardship actions would prevent them from becoming at risk. The program puts money into existing and new conservation activities that would maintain habitat considered critical to the survival and recovery of species in trouble. In the first year, the program helped develop more than 60 partnerships with First Nations, landowners, resource users, nature trusts, provinces, community-based wildlife societies, educational institutions and conservation organizations.

Federal stewardship projects have improved the habitat of

A red-winged blackbird on a cattail.

about 60 nationally endangered and threatened species, and more than 100 species which provinces have listed. The habitat stewardship program is partnership-based. The federal government designs and funds the program in conjunction with non-federal partners, who are charged with implementing it. The Wildlife Service's Clayton Rubec said the key to the program is that stewardship by individual landowners remains strictly voluntary.

"You can't take away their land or take away what they regard as rights to their land," he noted. "We're all collectively looking at mechanisms so we can work co-operatively with landowners."

Ranchers and farmers control much of Canada's remaining private land, and the future of the wildlife living on it. They don't like to be told what they should or should not do with it, and will dig in their heels when government or anybody else tries to wrest away control of their land. Traditionally, these individuals have strong historical, cultural and economic ties to the land. They pride themselves on taking care of it. They learn to identify and control weeds, and work with innovative partnership programs such as Alberta's Cows and Fish program to determine how to decrease their livestock's impact on streams and rivers, and promoting habitat on riparian areas. Many organizations, such as the Alberta Cattle Commission, have assumed leadership roles in educating their rural members on issues impacting their land. The Cross Conservation Area also has been a leader in offering evening and daylong workshops to educate landowners in eco-friendly land stewardship programs.

As with everything else in life, there are always a few bad actors on the stage. Some landowners permit excessive grazing, log indiscriminately and engage in other ecologically damaging practices. But, for the most part, farmers and ranchers have a tradition of looking after the land. That shouldn't be surprising,

A mule deer buck in snow.

Tuft of deer hair stuck on barbed wire fence.

considering what is at stake. "The nature of our business is to be good environmental stewards," says Ralph Nelson, a third-generation foothills rancher and chairman of the Municipal District of Foothills environment committee. "If you trash the land, you're not going to survive."

The concept of organized private land stewardship was popular in the United States long before hitting stride in Canada. Thousands of land trusts – entities established for the sole purpose of preserving a certain type of land in a specific area — exist in the U.S., compared to just 136 in Canada. They have a practical purpose – the long-term preservation of land – but emotional ties to the land also play a major role. "People need to have a sense they can protect what they grew up with," said Clayton Rubec. Although landowners have always been able to donate property to various governments and municipalities in Canada, he concedes many people choose not to because they don't trust governments at any level. Most land trusts are locally based, with leadership and membership drawn from the local community. The people with the answers may well be a straight-shooting friend or neighbor, not a stranger.

Most trusts concentrate on specific locations and types of ecosystems. For example, the focus of a trust in Ontario is on preserving land that can be seen from the Rideau Canal, a 200-kilometre chain of lakes, rivers and canals between Kingston and Ottawa. In Alberta, one of the more recent arrivals on the stewardship scene is the Southern Alberta Land Trust Society (SALTS), dedicated to preserving the environmental, productive, scenic and cultural values of Alberta's foothill and prairie regions, with emphasis on the Eastern Slopes of the Rocky Mountains.

The air outside was brisk and the stars shone brilliantly the evening of November 1st, 2000. Twenty-six people had left the warmth of their homes to gather in Belvedere House, the Cross Conservation Area's interpretive building. They were there to hear a presentation about SALTS, a High River-based, non-profit organization formed in 1998. It prides itself on being community backed and rancher driven.

It was apparent the audience represented a range of diverse backgrounds. There was a mix of new and old rural – city-employed acreage owners, ranchers and farmers – with the new clearly outnumbering the old. A leather-faced rancher in black felt cowboy hat and red-and-black checkered Mackinaw coat sat, arms folded across his chest, near the front of the room. Beside him was a man wearing slip-on shoes and sporty fleece vest, his grayish-brown hair flowing down his back tied in a ponytail with a red rubber band. Despite their obvious cultural differences, both men were brought together by a common interest: a desire to learn about preserving the integrity of their land. And they were hearing about it in a place that knows a thing or two about land stewardship.

Guy Greenaway, then SALTS director of education and

Mule deer in the Fall.

communications, challenged the crowd to think about what makes a certain landscape special. For example, what qualities contribute to the intrinsic value of the Cross Conservation Area? The responses were spoken with passion, loudly and in rapid-fire succession: beauty, animal life, watershed, habitat, recreation, peace and quiet, native grass and heritage. Longtime ranchers and farmers, Greenaway pointed out, hold dear the same values in their own land. But as they become older and approach retirement, they become torn over their land's future, especially if their own children have shown no interest in carrying on the operation. They come under intense pressure to sell the land for recreation, or for residential development. If that happens, the habitat, wildlife, watersheds and scenic splendour that they've worked hard to sustain would be negatively impacted, possibly even destroyed. The threat is becoming increasingly difficult to stop because, in most rural areas, the fair market value of the land is outpacing its true agricultural value.

Nowhere is that more evident than in the Cross Conservation Area. In 2001, the land had an agricultural value of $700 an acre and a minimum market value of $5,000 an acre. That year, nary an eyebrow was raised among realtors or residents when a nearby 3.2-acre plot of raw undeveloped land – complete with spectacular mountain view – sold for $251,000.

At Belvedere House that night, Greenaway explained that farmers and ranchers have several options that can enable them to counter the economic-driven threat to their land by becoming part of the "conservation solution." A conservation easement is one choice. An easement is a voluntary agreement between a landowner and a qualified easement holder such as SALTS, or any other qualified charitable-status organization. The easement puts restrictions on the type and amount of allowable development in order to preserve the land's natural character and agricultural potential. With a conservation easement, the landowner gives up certain rights – for example, the right to subdivide or participate in other environmentally harmful activities – while still retaining land title.

Easements are usually granted in perpetuity and remain with the land even when it's sold. Landowners benefit financially because they might qualify for significant income tax deduction, or they might be able to sell the easement to an eligible organization. With future development rights relinquished, the appraised value of a property with an easement on it might be reduced, leading to a reduction in capital gains when the land is sold or transferred. Easements can be tailored to specific landowners, but they aren't the sole benefactors. "This is not just being done for ranchers," Greenaway noted. "This is for the land."

Aldo Leopold, widely recognized as the father of modern-day wildlife management, had a special perspective on the concept of land preservation. "We abuse land because we regard it as a

Jenny Droppo, aged eight, holds a blue butterfly on her thumb.

commodity belonging to us," Leopold wrote in *A Sand County Almanac*. "When we see land as a community to which we belong, we may begin to use it with love and respect."

Although an increasing number of rural landowners have adopted this land ethic in recent years, not everyone buys into it. The land preservation movement is rife with stories of unjust irony. In Colorado, for example, a preservation-conscious landowner on one side of a scenic valley took out conservation easements ensuring his land will never be developed. On the valley's other side, another landowner subdivided and gleefully developed his property. As a marketing tool, he boasts to prospective buyers that they'll always have a terrific view because the land across from them will never be developed.

Although the developer no doubt has more jingle in his jeans, many would argue his selfless neighbor is far richer.

Sandy Cross's dream of children visiting the area to learn about nature came true.

Chapter 7
The Future

"We cannot change our past, but we can choose our future. Working together to restore the wild beauty, space, freedom and wildlife that have always shaped our collective dream of Canada, we can heal not just our land but ourselves."

Kevin Van Tighem, Canadian author and conservationist

"I think the Ann and Sandy Cross Conservation Area should stay in business for many, many more years from this day on."

Jaletha, student, Longview School

The area bounded by 5th and 8th avenues and 59th and 106th streets in New York City was considered a no-man's land in the mid 1800's. Located smack in the middle of Manhattan, the land could only be described as irregular, a mosaic of swamps, bluffs and rocky outcroppings. New Yorkers considered the area undesirable for private development. So what to do with it? After three years of debate, the state legislature in 1853 authorized the City of New York to acquire more than 700 acres (283 ha) of that land to create Central Park. In the next few years, 1,600 people, including Irish pig farmers and German gardeners, were displaced from crude shanties to clear the way for development of a sophisticated network of bridges, roads, carriage drives, promenades and equestrian paths

through the rolling meadows and trees. In 1863, the boundaries were expanded and the park grew to 843 acres (341 ha). Now, close to a century and a half later, Central Park is a world famous natural island in a churning sea of humanity.

People crystal ball gazing into the future of the Ann and Sandy Cross Conservation Area tend to draw comparisons with Manhattan's famous urban park. Is it a valid comparison? Strictly speaking, no. At this point at least, the 4,800-acre (1,943 ha) natural area in the Alberta foothills appears to have little chance of becoming Central Park North. The two places are just too different in all too many ways: flora and fauna, history and reason for being – habitat preservation, conservation education and controlled public use versus developed roads, bridges, landscaping and unlimited access. Whereas Central Park became a park because it was deemed unsuitable for development, the Cross project became a conservation area to save it from development that otherwise was inevitable.

Without question, however, the Cross area already bears some similarity to Central Park. The foothills conservation area indeed is a lush oasis in a desert of development. The major difference is that most of it is rural while Central Park is surrounded by development that is decidedly urban.

Visitors to the Cross Conservation Area often will stride to the highest hill — which gives them a clear view of the sprawling city

— and note with alarm that Calgary's boundary has spread to within one mile (1.6 km). When Sandy Cross began buying the land that became Rothney Farm back in 1945, the city was several miles distant. Calgary's population then was just a few thousand shy of 100,000. Now, it's expected to hit 1.25 million people by the year 2017, if not sooner. The forecast has fueled speculation the Cross Area eventually will be in Calgary. The possibility can't be ruled out completely, but it's highly unlikely. "The Cross Conservation Area is an incredible gift for future generations," says Calgary Alderman Linda Fox-Mellway, co-chairman of the joint City of Calgary-M.D. of Foothills intermunicipal committee. She represents Ward 14, a sprawling district that extends south into countryside the city has annexed from Foothills municipal district. Fox-Mellway says the city will avoid doing anything that might negatively impact the "very significant" conservation area.

In 1998, the city and M.D. prepared and approved an intermunicipal development plan, identifying Calgary's primary urban growth corridor as an 11-square-mile (28 sq. km) area straddling Highway 2 directly south of the city. The west boundary of the growth corridor is five miles (8 km) from the east boundary of the Conservation Area. "I can see the city being as far south as Okotoks, but not in my lifetime," says Harry Riva Cambrin, Foothills' municipal manager. "But I can't see the city going as far west as the Cross Area." Although Calgary has spread to within one

mile of the Conservation Area's northeast corner, it's stayed on the north side of Highway 22X. The city appears to be stalled there, at least for the foreseeable future. According to the intermunicipal plan, the primary urban growth corridor directly south of Calgary "provides the best opportunities for the most efficient and economical urban development to the south of the current city limits." It's expected the designated area will provide most of the city's land supply for 30 years.

Fox-Mellway noted that Fish Creek Provincial Park, which was quite rightfully welcomed as a great asset to the city when it opened in 1975, eventually presented significant transportation challenges to city council. The city had to abandon plans to make Bow Bottom Trail S.E. a major thoroughfare south through the park to service future residential subdivisions. As a result, Macleod Trail and Deerfoot Trail became traffic nightmares as major housing subdivisions were developed in the south part of Calgary. The Cross Area would present similar obstacles if the city were to grow towards it. It would be extremely difficult to develop transportation, sewer and water services around such a large chunk of undeveloped land. Fish Creek will serve as a constant reminder to city councils well into the future that having a major natural area within a city can lead to infrastructure problems.

Notwithstanding any future plans or thoughts the city might ever have regarding the Conservation Area, the project is protected by terms of a 99-year lease with the province. Until the lease expires on September 19, 2095, the allowable uses of the Cross Area will continue to be conservation, outdoor education, nature interpretation, habitat retention and habitat enhancement.

The more immediate challenge for the Cross Area is country acreages, which have spread like wildfire in that corner of the Municipal District of Foothills. The Conservation Area now has 700 houses within a three-mile (4.8 km) radius, half of them developed within the past five years. An exclusive acreage development is within a stone's throw of the public entrance in the northeast corner of the Cross Area. There's no sign that trend will abate in the near future. Quite the contrary. In years to come, as economic pressures continue to put the squeeze on traditional farmers and ranchers, it appears inevitable that the few larger land holdings remaining in the area will be developed as acreages.

That irks Ralph Nelson, a High River-area rancher who serves

The city of Calgary is rapidly spreading into the surrounding countryside.

as chairman of the M.D. of Foothills environment committee. "It really concerns me to see it carved up like this," said the former professional steer wrestler. He laments the fact that economics are driving the issue and deciding the fate of good range and farmland. Nelson is bothered that some farmers claim their operations can't survive if they aren't permitted to subdivide off pieces of land for acreage development. He doesn't buy that argument. "It's a sad commentary on the state of agriculture to think we have to carve off a piece of land to survive," Nelson said.

The sharp increase in acreage development has contributed to a major problem for wildlife. Mammals such as elk, moose, deer, coyote, cougar and bear have huge natural ranges. Barbed wire fences don't keep them in, but lack of habitat can keep them moving in search of some. Elk, bear, wolf and cougar migrate between winter and summer ranges. Younger animals move regularly to establish their own territories. Wildlife moves between the Conservation Area and neighboring lands to search for food, water, bedding areas and mates. Rather than move while fully exposed in open fields and clearings, wildlife prefer using natural travel routes known as corridors – an interconnected network of trees, willows, other natural cover and broken terrain that allows them to remain concealed from predators. Acreage development fragments this landscape. It forces wildlife to seek cover elsewhere, opening them up for harassment by people and domestic pets, or

death on area highways. Many supporters of the Cross Conservation Area believe it's time to act to ensure wildlife has sufficient travel corridors well into the future.

Darlene Lavender, former chairperson and five-year member of the board of the Sandy Cross Conservation Foundation, said the board has been concerned for many years that if wildlife corridors aren't kept open, animals that live on the Conservation Area and adjoining properties will become stranded in isolated pockets of habitat. Some travel routes used by large animals already have been blocked by subdivision development. Lavender believes landowners can't be forced by legislation to preserve wildlife corridors on their land. The regulatory "big stick" approach doesn't work, she added. When government tells landowners what to do with their private land, they resent it. Instead, protecting corridors must be seen as a voluntary decision, perhaps encouraged by incentives, financial or otherwise.

Larry Simpson, Alberta and Northern Region director of the Nature Conservancy of Canada, said establishing an effective network of wildlife corridors will require substantial financial commitment. Landowners, he says, may have to receive some sort of financial incentive before they voluntarily establish corridors on their property.

Significantly, an elderly woman who lives near the Conservation Area has told General Manager Jacquie Gilson that she's made provision in her will for a conservation easement that will ensure, in perpetuity, that wildlife have a travel corridor on her property. Other neighbors have expressed a similar intent. None have expected or requested any financial benefit in return. Interestingly, many neighbors and other rural residents are increasingly seeking advice from CCA staff regarding easements and other land management and conservation issues.

Darlene Lavender notes that people who move from the city to the country share many of the same values as longstanding farmers and ranchers. They didn't move out of the city to see gravel roads; they came to view wildlife and, hopefully, to live in harmony with it. Given the right incentives, she said, landowners would want to do the right thing to help wildlife. Their viewpoints on the issue must be sought early in the discussion, so a solution can be reached before it's too late for wildlife. "I like to think residents will share our concerns and keep wildlife populations viable," Lavender said. "I hope we'll get more creative about how to encourage people to allow corridors through their land, to see the value in it."

The M.D. of Foothills has taken a major step toward establishing wildlife corridors, not just near the Conservation Area but also throughout the municipality. The M.D.'s environment committee is spearheading a groundbreaking project to establish a computerized mapping system of potential wildlife corridors. The project is being done in conjunction with the University of Calgary,

John McKenzie, of Foothills Forage Co-op Association, demonstrates a machine for controlling weeds during a land stewardship education session beside Belvedere House.

University of Lethbridge and Agriculture and Agrifood Canada's Prairie Farm Rehabilitation Administration (PFRA).

Environment committee chairman Nelson said it would be difficult for Foothills council to establish planning policies to protect corridors until the municipality has a complete inventory of all areas which are important to wildlife. Nelson laments what he considers a common misconception that wildlife use only forests and riparian habitat along rivers and streams. "We need to preserve those areas, but there's also a need to preserve good agricultural lands," Nelson said. "Native grasslands are just as important to wildlife as a bunch of bush." Agricultural areas provide both habitat and feed to wildlife such as deer and elk, he added. Nelson suggested it might take tax incentives and "a strong political" will to convince landowners to preserve wildlife corridors.

The Cross Conservation Area took the issue directly to area residents in spring 2001 at a public meeting in nearby Priddis Community Hall, as part of the Conservation Matters series of special events. About 50 people showed up to hear environmental scientist Jake Herrero speak of the danger of people relegating wildlife to isolated "little islands" of habitat. For animals to survive, they need "a life-sustaining web of interconnecting core protected areas," he noted. The son of well-known grizzly bear biologist Stephen Herrero, Jake sounded like his father's son as he passionately described the problems that have developed in his hometown of Canmore.

Located just outside Banff National Park, the former coal-mining town has boomed in the past decade as outdoors enthusiasts rush to move closer to hiking, climbing, skiing and other activities in the Rocky Mountains. Canmore's population is expected to more than double – to 21,000 people — in the next several years. Housing and golf course developments now choke the Bow River Valley, dramatically changing the landscape. The boom has been like a giant vise squeezing out the wolves, grizzly bears, cougars, elk and other wildlife that used to move freely along the valley.

Although small wildlife corridors have been created, Herrero and other wildlife experts don't expect they'll be too effective because they fall below accepted minimum standards for length, width and hiding cover. The corridors were designed after most of the major development planning was already completed.

In 1996, students Lois Pittaway and Neil Gilson from the University of Calgary faculty of environmental design conducted a study on wildlife movement patterns in and around the Cross Conservation Area. The study identified potential wildlife corridors

Ralph Schmidt (foreground) and government wildlife biologist Pat Young examine a young elk captured on the Conservation Area before relocating it to Kananaskis Country.

and suggested four ways of ensuring they are preserved: through ongoing dialogue between planners and residents; continuing responsible land stewardship; taking conservation into consideration when planning new subdivisions; and by making use of the so called "landowner's tool chest" — long-term preservation options such as conservation easements, land donations and changes in zoning regulations.

General Manager Gilson told the meeting that Foothills Municipal District and neighbors of the Cross Area are in a good position to plan for unrestricted wildlife movements, because most of the land surrounding it hasn't been developed yet. "We have the chance to do something now, before it's too late," she said. Around the room, most people nodded their heads in silent agreement.

But the comment raised the ire of a longtime local resident who has ranched in the area for 60 years. He claimed it's wrong to ensure elk free movement in and out of the Conservation Area, because they habitually eat neighbours' crops and haystacks. The rancher said more should be done to reduce local elk populations, not make it easier for them to move around. He noted hunters could do a better job of reducing the elk numbers if only more local residents allowed hunting on their land. Vehicles kill more elk on area highways each year than bow hunters do in hunting season each autumn, he added.

Gilson didn't seem surprised at the outburst. Although she

A young elk in a chute at the trap on the Conservation Area prior to being relocated to Kananaskis Country.

115

sympathized with the rancher's present day concern, she suggested it's important for us to consider the future and to look at long-term solutions to wildlife issues rather than getting too caught up in present day problems. The rancher nodded in agreement. Gilson also pointed out that elk were identified as a potential problem early in the development of the Cross Area, and that measures have been taken to address the issue. One of those measures is a provincial government-operated elk enclosure that has been in use for the past several winters.

***

Light snow dusted the tan backs of four elk as they stood motionless in a plywood-lined corral on a part of the Ann and Sandy Cross Conservation Area that's closed to the public. It was late February 2001. Several people stood on a raised wooden walkway, poised to haze the elk towards a steel squeeze mechanism at the end of the chute. Government wildlife biologist Pat Young and technician Ralph Schmidt huddled to discuss how best to move the elk — one at a time and with as little stress as possible — from the corral into a waiting horse trailer. The trailer will be used to take the elk to their new homes in Kananaskis Country.

The elk – three young cows and a yearling bull — were the last of 123 elk captured on the Conservation Area that winter and relocated to other parts of Alberta. In three years of operating the trap, 285 elk have been captured and relocated to Kananaskis

Elk captured at Cross Conservation Area is released in Kananaskis Country.

Country and remote parts of west-central Alberta — areas where elk used to be more common and won't pose a problem to landowners. It's part of an effort to reduce the district's elk population from 400 to 200. Ideally, the government would like to trap and relocate 150 to 200 elk annually from the Conservation Area. Basically, reaching that target each year would keep pace with the calf crop, maintaining the population of the local herd at a manageable size. Young believes the region probably can support a total of 200 elk. A larger population will cause problems with elk munching crops of winter wheat and fall rye, and raiding haystacks of landowners who haven't erected fences.

The trapping process is done with the precision of a military maneuver. Schmidt is in charge of reconnaissance. He keeps close tabs on elk herds by scouting the area in his truck, and trading intelligence with farmers and ranchers such as Reg Rempel, who manages the Conservation Area's agricultural business. When elk declared surplus by the Fish and Wildlife Division move onto the Conservation Area, they're baited with hay into a four stage, 48-acre (19 ha) wooden enclosure culminating in a smaller wooden corral. Following the feed from compartment to compartment as they move progressively deeper into the enclosure, they don't even realize they're caught until Schmidt closes the door at the other end. The Rocky Mountain Elk Foundation and Alberta Conservation Association underwrite the cost of the trapping program. The forest

industry has provided costly sophisticated collars that have been affixed to some elk so their movements can be tracked with radio and GPS signals.

At a signal from Schmidt, the volunteer assistants on the walkway start waving long-handled curling brooms and poles to move the elk through the narrow chute toward the squeeze. The operation goes smoothly; all three young cows individually move into the squeeze without much encouragement from the herders above them. Young and Schmidt affix ear tags and pull out a few strands of hair, so that each animal's DNA can be recorded. After each animal is processed, the squeeze is opened and it trots into the trailer. The last elk, the bull, takes much more convincing before it reluctantly moves into the squeeze. A few minutes later, it too runs into the trailer. Another successful operation.

"This is all part of being good neighbours and it seems to be working," Young said.

***

Being good neighbours has always been important to the people behind the Cross Conservation Area, starting with Ann and Sandy themselves. Staff and foundation board members have worked hard to maintain a relationship with people who live in the area, and to help inform them on issues involved in living in a rural region. Their approach is friendly, non-confrontational and reflects a deep love of the land.

The foundation has managed the area with firm resolve, its deliberations regarding use and management reflecting a level of wisdom and sensitivity that future managers would be wise to emulate. In 1997, the board of directors adopted this five-year vision:

"Our vision is to manage the Ann and Sandy Cross Conservation Area to reflect the guiding principles by managing for ecological integrity, while showing environmental leadership and serving as a model for conservation."

On September 20, 1996, after Ann and Sandy donated an additional 2,800 acres (1,133 ha.), the foundation signed a new 99-year lease with the Alberta government. As the lessee, the Sandy Cross Conservation Foundation paid the province the grand total of one dollar in rent for the entire term of the lease.

Since its creation in 1987, change has not been a byword in the operation of the Conservation Area. But a provision in the lease allows for a major change after the year 2005. After December 31st of that year, a clause in the lease allows the province – in consultation with the Foundation – to withdraw up to 320 acres (130 ha) located on the periphery of the lands for purposes of establishing a public park. Former Foundation chairperson Darlene Lavender calls the clause a "safety valve," that would be activated only if there was considerable public interest in having less restricted access to a

Board of directors of Sandy Cross Conservation Foundation photographed at the annual general meeting, September 24, 2001. From left: Al Taylor, J. Sherrold Moore, Maureen Heffring (chair), Al Steingart, Darlene Lavender (past chair), Tom Beck (vice-chair) and Harold Millican. Missing are Ann and Sandy Cross and Rob Peters.

portion of the Conservation Area.

It's a safe bet that nobody directly involved in the Cross Area's present-day management will be around when the current lease expires in 2095. But foundation members and the project's many devoted supporters are confident not much will change after that time. They foresee support for the Conservation Area being passed on from generation to generation, ensuring continuation of the moral and political will needed to carry on the vision. "Long before the existing lease expires, succeeding generations will be seeking areas like the Cross Conservation Area," Darlene Lavender believes. "This is such a wonderful gift that it will be appreciated for a long time to come."

The project's ongoing and future success should be at least partially ensured by the composition of the board of the Sandy Cross Conservation Foundation. It includes representatives of the business community, area residents and other major partners, including the Alberta government and M.D. of Foothills. Ann and Sandy Cross each have a seat. Originator Tom Beck sits on the board while fellow originator George Crawford is chairman emeritus. The third originator, Ray Glasrud, was a board member before he moved to Saskatchewan in 2001. The board's makeup ensures that the various partners involved in the Cross Area's operations are kept up to date on issues and developments, and have a major say in future decisions.

Partnerships – past, present and future — are critical to the operation of the Cross Conservation Area. In addition to financial backing many partners provide, they also contribute moral and philosophical support for its goals and programs. The historic support shown by the M.D. of Foothills, Alberta government, Rocky Mountain Elk Foundation, Agriculture and Agrifood Canada, Calgary Foundation, Chevron Canada Resources and many other major longtime supporters is regularly reinforced by donations from many individuals and donors such as Toronto Dominion/Canada

Trust Friends of the Environment Foundation, Active Environmental Services, various school and education groups, Goodman McDougall and Associates Ltd., and Glacier Water. Environmental organizations such as the Central Rockies Wolf Project and the Yellowstone to Yukon Coalition provide useful information about issues pertinent to the Cross Area and its supporters.

"All our partnerships help us immensely," says Jacquie Gilson. "It really helps to keep in touch with other groups so that we're not reinventing the wheel. It gives us a chance to network while getting support and information for our programs. Our partners really help us deliver our mandate. We're extremely grateful for all that they do."

The value of those special partnerships was publicly recognized at a gala ceremony in Edmonton on June 12, 2002, when the Sandy Cross Conservation Foundation was honoured with Alberta's coveted Emerald Award in the education category. The award recognizes Albertans for outstanding achievements in projects that protect, preserve, enhance and sustain the environment. Nominations are judged on the basis of commitment to preservation, protection, enhancement or sustainability of the environment, and their positive, tangible and long-term impact on quality of air, water or land; preservation of biological diversity; and public or corporate attitudes toward the environment.

Board chairperson Maureen Heffring and general manager/executive director Jacquie Gilson attended the ceremony in the elegantly beautiful Francis Winspear Centre for Music. In accepting the heavy, emerald-green glass award, Gilson paid tribute to the generosity of Ann and Sandy Cross. She told the audience many other people deserve to share the honour. "Also on stage with me should be our board, staff and helpers past and present, taking credit for all their hard work and efforts over the last 10 years. Our volunteers deserve credit too. If they were here, they'd fill the stage and then some."

The Cross Area has garnered considerable public support in the local media, which has kept the public informed about major developments. Not surprisingly, considering the positive nature of Ann and Sandy's gift and the subsequent programs that have been developed, the coverage to date has all been positive in local newspapers and on radio and television.

Everyone who has been involved in the Cross Area since 1987 can only hope that future generations practice a land ethic that's as strong – even stronger, if that's possible — as those who came before them. With all their hearts, they hope their successors honor the vision of a man who put nature before riches, so that others could learn and be better for it. And they pray that the three original guiding principles – protecting wildlife habitat, offering conservation education and managing human use of the area by limiting access – will continue to serve as the foundation of the next lease, the one after that and all successive leases.

On September 24, 1996, at the ceremony to mark the expansion of the Ann and Sandy Cross Conservation Area, the crowd became respectfully quiet as a small, white-haired man stepped up to the podium. Sandy Cross's casual white windbreaker was partially zipped over his open necked sport shirt. A slight west wind ruffled his sparse hair. When the applause started, Sandy looked a little self-conscious, as if he was wondering why all these people were making such a fuss.

Sandy, then 82, stood silent for a moment while he scanned the crowd. Then he adjusted his glasses, and peered past the people to the rolling foothills that had drawn him to this special place more than a half-century earlier. When he finally spoke, Sandy's voice was soft but full of resolve. "I hope the guiding principles are still in effect here 100 years from now and 1,000 years from now."

There was no elaboration. None was needed. Sandy had said it all, sharing his dream in a few simple words that can never be changed by time, or interpreted in any way other than how he meant them that sunny fall day in 1996. The words will echo forever, a truth carried in the wind that blows through the fields and trees at the Ann and Sandy Cross Conservation Area.

And if the words are never forgotten, this unique piece of paradise will be preserved forever, its wild inhabitants kept secure while children laugh and learn. That's the way Sandy Cross always wanted it, and that's the way it should always be.

The sun sets on the Cross Conservation Area.

APPENDIX ONE
Common Flora and Fauna (Compiled by Olga Droppo)

Mammals (seen on Conservation Area)

Badger
Bat, Little Brown
Bear, Black
Beaver, Canada
Chipmunk, Least
Cougar
Coyote, Prairie
Deer, White-tailed
    Mule
Elk, Rocky Mountain
Fox, Red
Gopher, Northern Pocket
Hare, Snowshoe
Lynx
Moose, Northwestern
Mouse, Deer
Muskrat
Porcupine
Shrew, Masked
    Pygmy
Skunk, Striped
Squirrel, Red
    Richardson's Ground Squirrel
    13-lined Ground Squirrel
Vole, Red-backed
    Meadow
Weasel, Long-tailed
    Short-tailed

Birds

Double-crested Cormorant
Great Blue Heron
Snow Goose
Canada Goose
Wood Duck
Green-winged Teal
Mallard
Blue-winged Teal
Northern Shoveler
Gadwall
American Wigeon
Canvasback
Lesser Scaup
Common Goldeneye
Barrow's Goldeneye
Bufflehead
Hooded Merganser
Common Merganser
Bald Eagle
Northern Harrier
Sharp-shinned Hawk
Cooper's Hawk
Northern Goshawk
Broad-winged Hawk
Swainson's Hawk
Red-tailed Hawk
Rough-legged Hawk
Golden Eagle
American Kestrel
Merlin
Peregrine Falcon
Prairie Falcon
Gyrfalcon, gray morph
Gray Partridge
Ring-necked Pheasant
Grouse, Ruffed
    Sharp-tailed
Sora
American Coot

Sandhill Crane
Killdeer
Lesser Yellowlegs
Solitary Sandpiper
Spotted Sandpiper
Common Snipe
Franklin's Gull
Black Tern
Rock Dove
Mourning Dove
Great Horned Owl
Barred Owl
Great Gray Owl
Short-eared Owl
Northern Saw-whet Owl
Hummingbird
Belted Kingfisher
Yellow-bellied Sapsucker
Red-naped Sapsucker
Downy Woodpecker
Hairy Woodpecker
Northern Flicker
Pileated Woodpecker
Olive-sided Flycatcher
Western Wood-Pewee
Alder Flycatcher
Willow Flycatcher
Least Flycatcher
Eastern Phoebe
Say's Phoebe
Eastern Kingbird
Horned Lark
Purple Martin
Tree Swallow
Rough-winged Swallow

Cliff Swallow
Bank Swallow
Barn Swallow
Blue Jay
Gray Jay
Black-billed Magpie
American Crow
Common Raven
Black-capped Chickadee
Mountain Chickadee
Boreal Chickadee
Red-breasted Nuthatch
White-breasted Nuthatch
Brown Creeper
House Wren
Golden-crowned Kinglet
Ruby-crowned Kinglet
Mountain Bluebird
Townsend's Solitaire
Swainson's Thrush
Hermit Thrush
Veery
American Robin
Gray Catbird
American Pipit
Sprague's Pipit
Bohemian Waxwings
Cedar Waxwing
Northern Shrike
European Starling
Warbling Vireo
Red-eyed Vireo
Solitary Vireo
Tennessee Warbler
Orange-crowned Warbler

Yellow Warbler
Yellow-rumped Warbler
Northern Waterthrush
Ovenbird
Common Yellow-throat
Western Tanager
Rose-breasted Grosbeak
Lazuli Bunting
American Tree Sparrow
Chipping Sparrow
Clay-colored Sparrow
Vesper Sparrow
Savannah Sparrow
La Conte's Sparrow
Lincoln's Sparrow
Song Sparrow
White-throated Sparrow
White-crowned Sparrow
Dark-eyed Junco
Snow Bunting
Red-winged Blackbird
Western Meadowlark
Brewer's Blackbird
Brown-headed Cowbird
Baltimore Oriole
Rosy Finch
Pine Grosbeak
Red Crossbill
White-winged Crossbill
Common Redpoll
Pine Siskin
American Goldfinch
House Sparrow

Plants

Equisetaceae/Horsetail Family

Equisetum arvense L.	Common Horsetail
Equisetum laevigatum A.Br.	Smooth Horsetail
Equisetum variegatum Schleich.	Varigated Horsetail

Polypodiaceae/Fern Family

Cystopteris fragilis (L.) Bernh.	Fragile Fern
Pellaea glabella Mett. *ex* Kuhn	Smooth Cliff Break

Cupressaceae/

Juniperus communis L.	Common Juniper
Juniperus horizontalis Moench	Creeping Juniper

Pinaceae E/Pine Family

Picea glauca (Moench) Voss	White Spruce
Pinus contorta Loudon	Lodgepole Pine

Typhaceae/Cattail Family

Typha latifolia L.	Common Cattail

Sparganiaceae/Bur-reed Family

Sparganium angustifolium Michx.	Narrow-leaved Bur-reed

Potamogetonaceae/Pondweed Family

Potamogeton filiformis Pers.	Thread-leaved Pondweed
Potamogeton pusillus L.	Small-leaf Pondweed
Potamogeton strictifolius Benn.	Linear-leaved Pondweed

Juncaginaceae/Arrow-grass Family

Triglochin maritima L.	Seaside Arrow-grass
Triglochin palustris L.	Slender Arrow-grass

Gramineae/Grass Family

Agropyron dasystachyum (Hook.)Scribn.	Northern Wheat Grass
Agropyron pectiniforme R & S	Crested Wheat Grass
Agropyron repens (L.)Beauv.	Quack Grass
Agropyron smithii Rydb.	Western Wheat Grass
Agropyron trachycaulum (Link)Malte var. *trachycaulum*	Slender Wheat Grass
Agropyron trachycaulum (Link)Malte var. *unilaterale (*Cassidy)Malte	Awned Wheat Grass
Alopecurus aequalis Sobol.	Water Foxtail
Alopecuruspratensis L.	Meadow Foxtail
Avena fatua L.	Wild Oats
Beckmannia syzigachne (Steud.)Fern.	Slough Grass
Bouteloua gracilis (HBK)Lag.	Blue Grama
Bromus anomalus Rupr. *ex* Fourn.	Nodding Brome
Bromus ciliatus L.	Fringed Brome
Bromus inermis Leyss.	Awnless Brome
Bromus inermis ssp *pumpellianis* (Scribn.)Wagon	Northern Awnless Brome
Calamagrostis montanensis Scribn.	Plains Reed Grass
Calamovilfa longifolia (Hook.)Scribn.	Sand Grass
Danthonia californica Boland	California Oat Grass
Danthonia parryi Scribn.	Parry Oat Grass
Festuca scabrella Torr.	Rough Fescue
Glyceria grandis S.Wats. *ex* A.Gray	Tall Manna Grass
Glyceria striata (Lam.)A.S.Hitchc.	Fowl Manna Grass
Helictotrichon hookeri (Scribn.)	Hooker's Oat Grass
Hierochloe odorata (L.)Beauv.	Sweet Grass
Hordeum jubatum L.	Foxtail Barley
Koeleria macrantha (Ledeb.)j.a.Schultes F.	June Grass
Muhlenbergia cuspidata (Torr.)Rydb.	Plains Muhly
Panicum capillare L.	Witch Grass
Phalaris arundinacea L.	Reed Canary Grass
Phleum pratense L.	Timothy Grass
Poa pratensis L.	Kentucky Bluegrass

Schizachyrium scoparium (Michx.)Nees	Little Bluestem Grass
Stipa columbiana Macoun	Columbia Needle Grass
Stipa curtiseta (A.S.Hitchc)Barkworth	Western Porcupine Grass
Stipa viridula Trin.	Green Needle Grass

Cyperaceae/Sedge Family

Carex aquatilis Wahlenb.	Water Sedge
Carex aurea Nutt.	Golden Sedge
Carex bebbii Olney *ex* Fern.	Bebb's Sedge
Carex douglasii Boott	Douglas'Sedge
Carex filifolia Nutt.	Thread-leaved Sedge
Carex gynocrates Wormsk.	Northern Bog Sedge
Carex lanuginosa Michx.	Woolly Sedge
Carex obtusata Lilj.	Blunt-leaved Sedge
Carex praegracilis W.Boott	Graceful Sedge
Carex rostrata Stokes	Beaked Sedge
Carex sprengelii Dewey	Sprengel's Sedge
Eleocharis acicularis (L.)R. & S.	Needle Spike-rush
Eleocharis palustris (L.)R. & S.	Creeping Spike-rush
Scirpus microcarpus Presl	Small-fruited Bulrush
Scirpus acutus Muhl. *ex* Bigel or *validus* vahl.	Great or Commom Great Bulrush

Lemnaceae/Duckweed Family

Lemna minor L.	Common Duckweed

Juncaceae/Rush Family

Juncus balticus Willd.	Wire Rush
Juncus nodosus L.	Knotted Rush

Liliaceae/Lily Family

Allium cernuum Roth	Nodding Onion
Allium textile Nels. & Macbr.	Prairie Onion
Disporum trachycarpum (S.Wats.)B. & H.	Fairy-bells
Lilium philadelphicum L.	Western Wood Lily
Smilacina racemosa (L.)Desf.	False Solomon's-seal

Western Wood Lily.

Smilacina stellata (L.)Desf.	Star-flowered Solomon's-seal
Streptopus amplexifolius (L.)DC.	Twisted-stalk
Zigadenus elegans Pursh	White Camas
Zigadenus venenosus S.Wats	Death Camas

Iridaceae/Iris Family

*Sisyrinchium montanum*Greene	Blue-eyed Grass

Orchidaceae/Orchid Family

Corallorhiza maculata Raf.	Spotted Coral-root Orchid
Corallorhiza striata Lindl.	Striped Coral-root Orchid
Corallorhiza trifida Chatelain	Pale Coral-root Orchid
Cypripedium calceolus L.	Yellow Lady's-slipper Orchid
Habenaria hyperborea (L.)R.Br.	Northern Green Orchid
Habenaria obtusata (Pursh)Richards.	Blunt-leaved Orchid
Habenaria viridis (L.)R.Br.	Bracted Orchid
Listera borealis Morong	Northern Twayblade
Orchis rotundifolia Banks *ex* Pursh	Round-leaved Orchid

*Salicaceae/*Willow Family

Populus balsamifera L.	Balsam Poplar
Populus tremuloides Michx.	Trembling Aspen
Salix bebbiana Sarg.	Bebb's Willow
Salix discolor Muhl.	Pussy Willow
Salix glauca L.	Smooth Willow
Salix lucida Muhl.	Shining Willow
Salix lutea Nutt.	Yellow Willow

*Urticaceae/*Nettle Family

Urtica dioica L.	Common Nettle

*Santalaceae/*Sandalwood Family

Comandra umbellata (L.)Nutt.	Pale Comandra or Bastard Toadflax

*Polygonaceae/*Buckwheat Family

Eriogonum flavum Nutt.	Yellow Umbrella-plant
Polygonum arenastrum Jord. *ex* Bor.	Common or Yard Knotweed
Polygonum convolvulus L.	Wild Buckwheat or Bindweed
Polygonum erectum L.	Striate Knotweed
Polygonum lapathifolium L.	Pale Water Smartweed
Polygonum monspeliense Pers.	Rabbit-foot Knotweed
Polygonum viviparum L.	Bistort
Rumex ac	Sorrel
Rumex crispus L.	Curled Dock
Rumex maritimus L.	Golden Dock
Rumex occidentalis S.Wats.	Western Dock
Rumex triangulivalvis (Dans.)Rech.f.	Narrow-leaved Dock
Rheum rhapoticum	Garden Rhubarb

*Chenopodiaceae/*Goosefoot Family

Axyris amaranthoides L.	Russian Pigweed
Chenopodium album L.	Lamb's-quarters
Chenopodium gigantospermum Aellen	Maple-leaved Goosefoot
Chenopodium salinum Standl.	Oak-leaved Goosefoot
Monolepis nuttalliana (Schultes)Greene	Spear-leaved Goosefoot
Salsola kali L.	Russian Thistle

*Amaranthaceae/*Amaranth Family

Amaranthus retroflexus L.	Red-root Pigweed

*Caryophyllaceae/*Pink Family

Cerastium arvense L.	Field Mouse-ear Chickweed
Cerastium vulgatum L.	Glandular Mouse-ear Chickweed
Moehringia lateriflora (L.)Fenzl.	Blunt-leaved Sandwort
Silene cucubalis Wibel	Bladder Campion
Silene drummondii Hook.	Drummond's Catchfly
Silene noctiflora L.	Night-flowering Catchfly
Silene parryi (S.Wats.)C.L.Hitchc. & Maguire	Parry's Catchfly
Stellaria crassifolia Ehrh.	Fleshy Chickweed
Stellaria longifolia Muhl.	Long-leaved Chickweed
Stellaria longipes Goldie	Long-stalked Chickweed
Stellaria media (L.)Cyrill.	Common Chickweed

*Ceratophyllaceae/*Hornwort Family

Ceratophyllum demersum L.	Hornwort or Coontail

*Ranunculaceae/*Buttercup or Crowfoot Family

Actaea rubra (Ait.)Willd.	Baneberry
Anemone patens	Prairie Crocus
Anemone canadensis L.	Canada Anemone
Anemone cylindrica A.Gray	Long-fruited Anemone
Anemone multifida Poir.	Cut-leaved Anemone
Anemone riparia Fern.	Tall Anemone
Clematis occidentalis (Hornem.)DC.	Purple Clematis
Delphinium bicolor Nutt.	Low Larkspur
Delphinium glaucum S.Wats.	Tall Larkspur
Ranunculus abortivus L.	Small-flowered Buttercup

Ranunculus acris L.	Tall Buttercup
Ranunculus aquatilis L.	White Water Buttercup
Ranunculus cardiophyllus Hook.	Heart-leaved Buttercup
Ranunculus circinatus Hook.	White Water Buttercup
Ranunculus cymbalaria Pursh	Seaside or Creeping Buttercup
Ranunculus glaberrimus Hook.	Early Buttercup
Ranunculus gmelinii DC.	Yellow Water Buttercup
Ranunculus inamoenus Greene	Graceful Buttercup
Ranuncukus macounii Btitt.	Macoun's Buttercup
Ranunculus pedatifidus J.E.Smith	Northern Buttercup
Ranunculus sceleratus L.	Celery-leaved Buttercup
Thalictrum venulosum Trel.	Veiny Meadow Rue

*Fumariaceae/*Fumitory Family
Corydayis aurea Willd.	Golden Corydalis

*Cruciferae/*Mustard Family
Arabis drummondii A.Gray	Drummond's Rock Cress
Arabis glabra (L.)Bernh.	Tower Mustard
Arabis hirsuta (L.) Scop.	Hirsute Rock Cress
Arabis holboellii Hornem.	Reflexed Rock Cress
Brassica campestris L.	Rape
Capsella bursa-pastoris (L.)Medic.	Shepherd's-purse
Cardamine pensylvanica Muhl.	Btter Cress
Descurainia pinnata (Walt.)Britt.	Green Tansy Mustard
Descurainia richardsonii (Sweet)O.E.Schulz	Grey Tansy Mustard
Descurainia sophia (L.)Webb	Flixweed
Diplotaxis muralis (L.)DC.	Sand Rocket
Draba nemorosa L.	Annual Draba or Whitlow-grass
Erucastrum gallicum (Willd.)Schulz	Dog Mustard
Erysimum cheiranthoides L.	Wormseed Mustard
Erysimum inconspicuum (S.Wats.)MacM.	Small-flowered Rocket
Lepidium densiflorum Schrad.	Common Peppergrass
Neslia paniculata (L.)Desv.	Ball Mustard
Rorippa palustris (L.)Besser	Yellow Cress

Sisymbrium altissimum L.	Tumbling Mustard
Sisymbrium loeselii L.	Tall Hedge Mustard
Thlaspi arvense L.	Pennycress or Stinkweed

*Saxifragaceae/*Saxifrage Family
Heuchera richardsonii R.Br.	Richardson's Alumroot
*Mitella nuda*L.	Bishop's-cap or Mitrewort

*Parnassiaceae/*Grass-of-Parnassus Family
Parnassia palustris L.	Northern Grass-of-parnassus

*Grossulariaceae/*Currant or Gooseberry Family
Ribes americanum Mill.	Wild Black Currant
Ribes hudsonianum Richards.	Wild Black Currant
Ribes oxyacanthoides L.	Wild Gooseberry
Ribes triste Pall.	Wild Red Currant

*Rosaceae/*Rose Family
Agrimonia striata Michx	Agrimony
Amelanchier alnifolia Nutt.	Saskatoon
*Cotoneaster acutifolia*Turez.	Cotoneaster
Fragaria virginiana Duchesne	Strawberry
Geum aleppicum Jacq.	Yellow Avens
Geum macrophyllum Willd.	Large-leaved Yellow Avens
Geum rivale L.	Purple or Water Avens
Geum triflorum Pursh	Three-flowered Avens or Old Man's Whiskers
Potentilla anserina L.	Silverweed
Potentilla arguta Pursh	WhiteCinquefoil
Potentilla bipinnatifida Dougl. *ex* Hook.	Plains Cinquefoil
Potentilla concinna Richards.	Early Cinquefoil
Potentilla fruticosa L.	Shrubby Cinquefoil
Potentilla gracilis Dougl. *ex* Hook.	Graceful Cinquefoil
Potentilla hippiana Lehm.	Woolly Cinquefoil
Potentilla hookeriana Lehm.	Hooker's Cinquefoil
Potentilla norvegica L.	Rough Cinquefoil

Wild rose.

Potentilla pensylvanica L.	Prairie Cinquefoil
Potentilla rivalis Nutt.	Brook Cinquefoil
Prunus virginiana L.	Choke Cherry
Rosa acicularis Lindl.	Prickly Rose
Rosa arkansana Porter	Prairie Rose
Rosa woodsii Lindl.	Common Wild Rose
Rubus idaeus L.	Wild Red Rasperry
Rubus pubescens Raf.	Dewberry or Running Raspberry
Sorbus aucuparia L.	European Mountain Ash or Rowan Tree
Spiraea betulifolia Pallas	White Spirea or Meadowsweet

Leguminosae/Pea Family

Astragalus aboriginum Richards.	Indian Milk Vetch
Astragalus americanus (Hook.)M.E.Jones	American Milk Vetch
Astragalus crassicarpus Nutt.	Ground Plum or Buffalo Bean
Astragalus dasyglottis Fisch. *ex* DC.	Purple Milk Vetch
Astragalus drummondii Dougl. *ex* Hook	Drummond's Milk Vetch
Astragalus striatus Nutt.	Ascending Milk Vetch
Astragalus tenellus Pursh	Loose-flowered Milk Vetch
Caragana arborescens Lam.	Caragana
Glycyrrhiza lepidota (Nutt.)Pursh	Wild Licorice
Hedysarum alpinum L.	Alpine Hedysarum
Hedysarum sulphurescens Rudb.	Yellow Hedysarum
Lathyrus ochroleucus Hook.	Cream Peavine
Lotus corniculatus L.	Bird's-foot Trefoil
Lupinus sericeus Pursh	Silky Lupine
Medicago lupulina L.	Black Medick
Medicago sativa L.	Alfalfa
Melilotus alba Desr.	White Sweet Clover
Melilotus officinalis (L.)Lam.	Yellow Sweet Clover
Onobrychis viciifolia Scop.	Sainfoin
Oxytropis deflexa (Pall.)DC.	Reflexed Locoweed
Oxytropis monticola A.Gray	Late Yellow Locoweed
Oxytropis sericea Nutt.	Early Yellow Locoweed
Oxytropis splendens Dougl. *ex* Hook.	Showy Locoweed
Petalostemon purpureum (Vent.)Rydb.	Purple Prairie Clover
Psoralea esculenta Pursh	Indian Bread-root
Thermopsis rhombifolia (Nutt.)Richards.	Golden Bean
Trifolium hybridum L.	Alsike Clover
Trifolium prarense L.	Red Clover
Trifolium repens L.	White or Dutch Clover
Vicia americana Muhl.	American Vetch
Vicia cracca L.	Tufted Vetch

Geraniaceae/Geranium Family

Erodium cicutarium (L.)L'Her.	Stork's-bill
Geranium richardsonii Fisch. & Trautv.	White Geranium
Geranium viscosissimum Fisch. & Mey.	Sticky Purple Geranium

Linaceae/Flax Family

Linum lewisii Pursh	Wild Blue Flax

Polygalaceae/Milkwort Family

Polygala senega L.	Seneca-root

Euphorbiaceae/Spurge Family

Euphorbia esula L.	Leafy Spurge

Callitrichaceae/Water-Starwort Family

Callitriche verna L.	Vernal Water-starwort

Violaceae/Violet Family

Viola adunca L.E.Smith	Early Blue Violet
Viola canadensis L.	Western Canada Violet
Viola nephrophylla Greene	Bog Violet
Viola nuttallii Pursh	Yellow Prairie Violet

Elaeagnaceae/Oleaster Family

Elaeagnus commutata Bernh. *ex* Rydb.	Wolf Willow or Silver-berry
Shepherdia canadensis (L.)Nutt.	Canadian Buffalo-berry
Syringa persica L. var *villosa*	Persian or Late Lilac
Syringa vulgaris L.	Common Lilac

Onagraceae/Evening Primrose Family

Circaea alpina L.	Enchanter's nightshade
Epilobium angustifolium L.	Fireweed
Epilobium ciliatum Raf.	Northern Willowherb
Epilobium glandulosum (Lehm.)Hock & Raven	Glandular Willowherb
Epilobium palustre L.	Marsh Willowherb
Gaura coccinea Pursh	Scarlet Butterfly-weed
Oenothera biennis L.	Yellow Evening Primrose

Haloragaceae/Water-milfoil Family

Myriophyllum exalbescens Fern.	Spiked Water-milfoil
Myriophyllum verticillarum L.	Water-milfoil

Hippuridaceae/Mare's-tail Family

Hippuris vulgaris L.	Mare's-tail

Umbelliferae/Carrot Family

Carum carvi L.	Caraway
Cicuta maculata L.	Water Hemlock
Heracleum lanatum Michx.	Cow Parsnip
Osmorhiza depauperata Philippi	SweetCicely
Sanicula marilandica L.	Snake-root
Zizia aptera (A.Gray)Fern.	Heart-leaved Alexander or Meadow parsnip

Cornaceae/Dogwood Family

Cornus canadensis L.	Bunchberry
Cornus stolonifera Michx.	Red Osier Dogwood

Pyrolaceae/Wintergreen Family

Moneses uniflora (L.)A.Gray	One-flowered Wintergreen
Orthilia secunda (L.)House	One-sided Wintergreen
Pyrola asarifolia Michx.	Common Pink Wintergreen

Ericaceae/Heath Family

Arctostaphylos uva-ursi (L.)Spreng.	Common Bearberry

Primulaceae/Primrose Family

Androsace septentrionalis L.	Fairy Candelabra
Dodecatheon conjugens Greene	Mountain Shooting Star
Dodecatheon pulchellum (Raf.)Merr.	Saline Shooting Star
Lysimachia ciliata L.	Fringed Loosestrife

Gentianaceae/Gentian Family

Gentiana affinis Griseb.	Prairie Gentian
Gentianella amarella (L.)Borner	Felwort

Apocynaceae/Dogbane Family

Apocynum androsaemifolium L.	Spreading Dog

Polemoniaceae/Phlox Family

Collomia linearis Nutt.	Collomia
Phlox hoodii Richards.	Moss Phlox

Paintbrush.

Boraginaceae/Borage Family

Cynoglossum officinale L.	Hound's-tongue
Hackelia americana (A.Gray)Fern.	American Stickseed
Hackelia floribunda (Lehm.)I.M.Johnston	Large-flowered Stickseed
Lappula squarrosa (Retz.)Dumort.	Blue-bur
Lithospermum incisum Lehm.	Narrow-leaved or Fringed Puccoon
Lithospermum ruderale Lehm.	Woolly Gromwell

Mertensia paniculata (Ait.)G.Don.	Tall Mertensia or Lungwort
Plagiobothrys scouleri (H. & A.)Johnston	Plagiobothrys
Symphytum officinale L.	Comfrey

Verbenaceae/Vervain Family

Verbena bracteata Lag. & Rodr.	Carpet Vervain

Labiatae/Mint Family

Agastache foeniculum (Pursh)Ktze	Giant Hyssop
Galeopsis tetrahit L.	Hemp Nettle
Mentha arvensis L.	Wild Mint
Monarda fistulosa L.	Wild Bergamot or Horse Mint
Scutellaria galericulata L.	Skullcap
Stachys palustris L.	Hedge Nettle

Solanaceae/Nightshade Family

Solanum triflorum Nutt.	Wild Tomato

Scrophulariaceae/Figwort Family

Castilleja lutescens (Greenm.)Rydb.	Yellow Paint-brush
Castilleja miniata Dougl. *ex* Hook.	Red Paint-brush
Linaria vulgaris Hill	Butter-and-eggs or Toad-flax
Orthocarpus luteus Nutt.	Owl-clover
Pedicularis bracteosa Benth.	Western Lousewort
Pedicularis groenlandica Retz.	Red Elephant Head
Penstemon gracilis Nutt.	lilac-flowered Beard-tongue
Penstemon nitidus Dougl. *ex* Benth.	Smooth Blue Beard-tongue
Veronica americana (Raf.)Schw.	American Brooklime
Veronica peregrina L.	Wandering or Hairy Veronica

Orobanchaceae/Broom-rape Family

Orobanche fasciculata Nutt.	Clustered Broomrape

Plantaginaceae/Plantain Family

Plantago major L.	Common Plantain

*Rubiaceae/*Madder Family

Galium boreale L.	Northern Bedstraw
Galium trifidum L.	Small Bedstraw
Galium triflorum Michx.	Sweet-scented Bedstraw

*Caprifoliaceae/*Honeysuckle Family

Linnaea borealis L.	Twin-flower
Lonicera dioica L. var. *glaucescens* (Rydb.)Butters.	Twining Honeysuckle
Lonicera tartarica L.	Tarterian Honeysuckle
Symphoricarpos albus (L.)Blake	Snowberry
Symphoricarpos occidentalis Hook.	Buckbrush
Viburnum edule (Michx.)Raf.	Low-bush Cranberry or Mooseberry

*Dipsacaceae/*Teasel Family

Knautia arvensis (L.)Duby	Field Scabious or Blue Buttons

*Campanulaceae/*Bluebell Family

Campanula rapunculoides L.	Garden Bluebell
Campanula rotundifolia L.	Bluebell or Harebell

*Compositae/*Composite Family

Achillea millefolium L.	Common Yarrow
Agoseris glauca (Pursh)Raf.	Yellow False Dandelion
Antennaria anaphaloides Rydb.	Tall Pussytoes
Antennaria aprica Greene	Green-leaved Pussytoes
Antennaria parvifolia Nutt.	Small-leaved Pussytoes
Arctium minus (Hill)Bernh.	Common Burdock
Arnica chamissonis Less ssp *foliosa* (Nutt.)	Maguire Leafy Arnica
Arnica cordifolia Hook.	Heart-leaved Arnica
Artemisia absinthium L.	Wormwood or Absinthe
Artemisia biennis Willd.	Biennial Sage or Sagewort
Artemisia campestris L.	Plains Sage or Sagewort
Artemisia dracunculus L.	Dragonwort
Artemisia frigida Willd.	Pasture Sage or Sagewort
Artemisia longifolia Nutt.	Long-leaved Sage or Sagewort

Arnica.

Artemisia ludoviciana Nutt.	Prairie Sage or Sagewort
Aster ascendens Lindl.	Western Aster
Aster borealis (T. & G.)Prov.	Northern Aster
Aster campestris Nutt.	Meadow Aster
Aster ciliolatus Lindl.	Lindley's Aster
Aster conspicuus Lindl.	Showy Aster
Aster ericoides L.	Tufted White Prairie Aster
Aster falcatus Lindl.	Creeping White Prairie Aster
Aster hesperius A.Gray	Western Willow Aster
Aster laevis L.	Smooth Aster
Aster subspicatus Nees	Leafy-bracted Aster
Bidens cernua L.	Nodding Beggar-ticks
Cirsium arvense (L.)Scop.	Creeping or Canada Thistle
Cirsium flodmanii (Rydb.)Arthur	Flodman's Thistle
Cirsium undulatum (Nutt.)Spreng.	Wavy-leaved Thistle
Cirsium vulgare (Savi)Ten.	Bull Thistle
Crepis tectorum L.	Annual Hawksbeard
Erigeron caespitosus Nutt.	Tufted Fleabane

Erigeron glabellus Nutt.	Smooth Fleabane
Erigeron peregrinus (Pursh)Greene	Wandering Fleabane
Erigeron speciosus (Lindl.)DC.	Showy Fleabane
Gaillardia aristata Pursh	Gaillardia
Helianthus maximilianii Schrad.	Narrow-leaved Sunflower
Helianthus subrhomboideus Rydb.	Rhombic-leaved Sunflower
Heterotheca villosa (Pursh)Shinners	Golden Aster
Hieracium umbellatum L.	Narrow-leaved Hawkweed
Lactuca pulchella (Pursh)DC.	Common Blue Lettuce
Liatris punctata Hook.	Blazing Star
Matricaria matricarioides (Less.)Porter	Pineapple-weed
Petasites palmatus (Ait.)A.Gray	Palmate-leaved Coltsfoot
Petasites sagittatus (Pursh)A.Gray	Arrow-leaved Coltsfoot
Petasites vitifolius Greene	Vine-leaved Coltsfoot
Senecio canus Hook.	Prairie Groundsel
Senecio congestus (R.Br.)DC.	Marsh Ragwort or Groundsel
Senecio integerrimus Nutt.	Terminal-flowered Groundsel
Senecio pauperculus Michx.	Balsam Groundsel
Senecio vulgaris L.	Common Groundsel
Solidago gigantea Ait.	Giant Goldenrod
Solidago missouriensis Nutt.	Low Goldenrod
Solidago nemoralis Ait.	Showy Goldenrod
Solidago rigida L.	Stiff Goldenrod
Sonchus arvensis L.	Perennial Sow Thistle
Sonchus asper (L.)Hill	Annual or Spiny Sow Thistle
Sonchus uliginosus Bieb.	Perennial Sow Thistle
Taraxacum officinale Weber	Common Dandelion
Tragopogon dubius Scop.	Common Goat's-beard
Tragopogon pratensis L.	Goat's-beard

A wood frog hangs out in the pond, surrounded by seeds in parachute stage.

Amphibians
Salamander, Tiger
Frog, Boreal Chorus
      Wood

APPENDIX TWO
Key Early Supporters

Ann and Sandy Cross

Alberta Government

Husky Oil

George Crawford

Chevron Canada Resources

Amoco Canada Petroleum (now BP Canada Energy Company)

ATCO Ltd. and Canadian Utilities Ltd.

Shell Canada Ltd.

Joy Harvie MacLaren

Mobil Oil (now Exxon Canada Limited)

Norcen Energy Resources

Paramount Resources Ltd.

The Kahanoff Foundation

Chauvco Resources ltd.

Canadian Occidental Petroleum Ltd.

Alberta Recreation, Parks and Wildlife Foundation

Trimac Ltd.

TransCanada Pipelines

Gulf Canada Resources Ltd.

Nickle Family Foundation

Petro-Canada

Richard Scheller and Carol Poffenroth

TransAlta Utilities Corp.

Alberta Energy Company Ltd.

Carthy Foundation

DEKALB Energy Foundation

A.H. Marsh

Sceptre Resources Ltd.

Unocal Canada Ltd.

Canadian Hunter Exploration Ltd.

Home Oil Company Ltd. (now Anderson Exploration Ltd.)

PanCanadian Petroleum Ltd.

Renaissance Energy Ltd.

Suncor Inc.

Rosenberg/Goldstein Foundation

APPENDIX 3
Land Stewardship Resources

Sandy Cross Conservation Foundation/Ann and Sandy Cross
Conservation Area
Box 20, Site 23, RR 8
Calgary, Alberta   T2J 2T9
Tel: (403) 931-9001
Fax: (403) 931-2726
Email: info@crossconservation.org
Website (with links to other sites): www.crossconservation.org

Habitat Stewardship Program Secretariat
Environment Canada, Canadian Wildlife Service
Place Vincent Massey, 3rd floor
351 St. Joseph Blvd.
Hull, Quebec   K1A 0H3
Tel: (819) 953-4068
Fax: (819 994-4445

Ecological Gifts Secretariat
Canadian Wildlife Service
Environment Canada
Ottawa, Ontario   K1A 0H3
Tel: (800) 668-6767
Fax: (819) 953-3575

Nature Conservancy of Canada
110 Eglington Avenue West, Fourth Floor
Suite 400
Toronto, Ontario   M4R 1A3
Tel: (416) 932-3202
Toll free: 1-800-465-0029
Fax: (416) 932-3208
Email: nature@natureconservancy.ca
Web site: www.natureconservancy.ca

Ducks Unlimited Canada
Oak Hammock Marsh Interpretive Centre
Stonewall, Manitoba   R0C 2Z0
Tel: (204) 467-3000
Fax: (204) 467-9028
Email: webfoot@ducks.ca

Land Stewardship Centre of Canada
17503 45th Avenue
Edmonton, Alberta   T6M 2N3
Tel: (780) 483-1885
Fax: (780) 486-9599
Email: lsc@landstewardship.org
Website: www.landstewardship.org

Rocky Mountain Elk Foundation
P.O. Box 940
Rocky Mountain House, Alberta   T0M 1T0
Tel: (403) 845-6492
Fax: (403) 845-2410
Email: rmefc@rttinc.com

Southern Alberta Land Trust Society
P.O. Box 45016
High River, Alberta   T1V 1R7
Toll-free: 1-877-999-7258
Tel: (403) 652-4784
Fax: (403) 652-4786
Email: salts@telusplanet.net
Website: www.salts-landtrust.org

Alberta Conservation Association
P.O. Box 40027
Baker Centre Postal Outlet
Edmonton, Alberta   T5J 4M9
Tel: (403) 427-5192
Fax: (403) 422-6441

Alberta Fish and Game Association
6924 104 Street
Edmonton, Alberta   T6H 2L7
Tel: (780) 437-2342
Fax: (780) 438-6872
Email: office@afga.org

Calgary Zoological Society
1300 Zoo Road N.E.
P.O. Box 3036, Station B
Calgary, Alberta   T2m 4R8
Tel: (403) 232-9300
Fax: (403) 237-7582

The Land Trust Alliance
Suite 400 - 1331 H Street N.W.
Washington, DC
U.S.A.
20005-1147
Tel: (202) 638-4725
Fax: (202) 638-4730
Website: www.lta.org

Recommended Reading

Canada Customs and Revenue Agency (formerly Revenue Canada). 1997. *Registering a Charity for Income Tax Purposes*. T4063(E) Rev. 972780. Ottawa, ON.

Curthoys, Lesley Patricia. 1998. *For the Love of Alberta: Ways to Save Your Natural Heritage: Private Conservancy Guide for Alberta*. Federation of Alberta Naturalists, Edmonton, AB.

Diehl, Janet and Thomas S. Barrett. 1988. *The Conservation Easement Handbook: Managing land conservation and historic preservation easement programs*. Land Trust Alliance. Washington, D.C.

Environment Canada. *Ecological Gifts: Implementing Provisions of the Income Tax Act of Canada* (Revised May 1, 1998). Environment Canada, Canadian Wildlife Service. Ottawa, ON. (latest information on website: www.cws-scf.ec.gc.ca/ecogifts

Findlay, Barbara and Ann Hillyer. 1994. *Here Today, Here Tomorrow: Legal Tools for the Voluntary Protection of Private Land in British Columbia*. West Coast Environmental Law Research Foundation. Vancouver, BC.

Greenaway, Guy (Ed.) 2000. *Preserving Working Ranches in the Canadian West*. Southern Alberta Land Trust Society, the Land Conservancy of British Columbia and the Sonoran Institute. High River, AB.

Hilts, Stewart and Ron Reid. 1993. *Creative Conservation: A Handbook for Ontario Land Trusts*. Federation of Ontario Naturalists. Don Mills, ON.

Kwasniak, Arlene. 1996. *Conservation Easement Guide for Alberta*. Environmental Law Centre. Edmonton, AB.

Montana Land Reliance and Land Trust Exchange. 1982. *Private Options: Tools and Concepts for Land Conservation*. Island Press. Covelo, CA.

Pauley, Glenn. 1996. *Landowner Attitudes Toward the Use of Conservation Easements to Preserve Wildlife Habitat and Agricultural Land*. Faculty of Environmental Design, University of Calgary. Calgary, AB.

SALTS (Southern Alberta Land Trust Society). 2000. *A Landowners Guide to Conservation Easements*. High River, AB.

SALTS (Southern Alberta Land Trust Society). 2000. *Establishing a Land Trust: The Experience of the Southern Alberta Land Trust Society*. High River, AB.

The Nature Conservancy of Canada. 2000. *Investing in Our Natural Heritage: A Conservation Tool Chest for Landowners*. 1-877-262-1253.

The Land Trust Alliance. 1990. *Starting a Land Trust: A Guide to Forming a Land Conservation Organization*. Washington, DC.

The Land Trust Alliance. 1997. *The Standards and Practices Guidebook: An operating manual for land trusts*. Washington, DC.

INDEX